T0268001

IMAGINATION

A Manifesto

ALSO BY RUHA BENJAMIN

Viral Justice: How We Grow the World We Want (2022)

*Race After Technology: Abolitionist Tools
for the New Jim Code* (2019)

*Captivating Technology: Race, Carceral Technoscience, and
Liberatory Imagination in Everyday Life* (ed.) (2019)

*People's Science: Bodies and Rights on the
Stem Cell Frontier* (2013)

IMAGINATION

A Manifesto

RUHA BENJAMIN

W. W. NORTON & COMPANY
Independent Publishers Since 1923

Copyright © 2024 by Ruha Benjamin

All rights reserved
Printed in the United States of America
First Edition

For information about permission to reproduce selections from this
book, write to Permissions, W. W. Norton & Company, Inc.,
500 Fifth Avenue, New York, NY 10110

For information about special discounts for bulk purchases, please
contact W. W. Norton Special Sales at specialsales@wwnorton.com or
800-233-4830

Manufacturing by Lakeside Book Company
Production manager: Delaney Adams

ISBN 978-1-324-02097-4

W. W. Norton & Company, Inc., 500 Fifth Avenue, New York, N.Y. 10110
www.wwnorton.com

W. W. Norton & Company Ltd., 15 Carlisle Street, London W1D 3BS

1 2 3 4 5 6 7 8 9 0

Dream a little before you think.

—Toni Morrison

The map to a new world is in the imagination.

—Robin D. G. Kelley

CONTENTS

PREFACE

IMAGINATION, BY DEFINITION, takes many different forms. Still, *Merriam-Webster Dictionary* comes in handy: "The act or power of forming a mental image of something not present to the senses or never before wholly perceived in reality." In this book, however, I refuse to police the parameters of imagination. I want more than anything for your imagination to run wild.

In that spirit, my use of the word is undisciplined, promiscuous, and porous. Although a key term in my academic field of sociology is *sociological imagination*—referring to the capacity to link individuals' personal problems with broader social processes—my approach here is more unruly. I go back and forth between imagination and imaginaries—conceptual kin, related but not identical. Although a bit jargony as a noun, an *imaginary* refers to collective projections of a desirable and feasible future. I find myself invoking imaginaries when I want to cast a critical light on the imposition of a dominant imagination that presents itself as appealing and universal. You'll see, too, that I refer to imagination interchangeably with dreams and dreaming, ideas and ideologies. I invoke stories and speculation as surrogates, playing and poetry as proxies, and myths, visions, and narratives all as riffs on the imagination.

In most cases, I am implying the idea of a *collective* imagination, as when we imagine different worlds together, writing shared stories and plotting futures in which we can all flourish. But this "collecting" of our imaginations is not always a good thing, as when the powers that be endeavor to download their dreams from on high. We must learn to protect our imaginations.

"Imagination doesn't erase nightmares," says author Imani Perry, "but it can repurpose them with an elaborate sense-making or troublemaking." And, if imagination can lead to troublemaking, is it any wonder, then, that those in power work tirelessly to squash us from having radical imaginations that dare to envision a world in which everyone can thrive?

My conceptual unruliness is sure to frustrate those desiring discipline, but perhaps it is a balm for those avoiding rigor mortis.

If, as the great anticolonial writer Aimé Césaire put it, "poetic knowledge is born in the great silence of scientific knowledge," then I invite you, as a reader, writer, and dreamer, to bring your own poetic understanding of *all* that imagination is and can be.

IMAGINATION

A Manifesto

CUTTING SCHOOL

———

ONCE A WEEK in fifth grade, I cut school. Or so it seemed. On Fridays, I jumped out of bed and threw on the clothes I had laid out the night before, then raced to the kitchen to pour a big bowl of Cheerios. Cereal devoured, I huffed and puffed, waiting for my mom to get my little brother, Jamal, ready and then open the front door, so I could race up the block to South Conway Elementary School.

Arriving just as the 8:00 a.m. bell rang, I didn't scurry in after the other kids, their backpacks bouncing up and down in the crowded halls. Instead, I boarded a bus waiting just under the flagpole and, together with a handful of other students, almost all of whom were white, headed to a portable classroom trailer at the back of the nearby middle school.

There we entered another world—no ringing bells telling us to move to another class, no sitting at desks lined up in rows, no stuffing ourselves with information to be regurgitated on tests. We cut school. Or so I thought.

I spent what I considered "Freedom Fridays" in the Pelican

Program for students who, I would only later learn, were labeled "gifted and talented." At the time, it seemed to me that adults had decided I could have fun once a week. Or perhaps they just wanted us out of their hair. This was, after all, fifth grade. I was the troublesome kid who got up in the middle of class to shush students making noise in the hallway, to the chagrin of the *actual* teacher.

The coolest part of cutting school was that my best friends, Qima and Mary, were in the Pelican Program too. We were the only Black students selected from our majority white school, where Black children made up about 30 percent. Everything else from those days is a blur. All I remember was the three of us floating together in a bubble of Black Girl Magic before it was a hashtag. We danced and sang and created poems and plays. Freedom Fridays were full of expressiveness, friendship, and play.

The scholar Imani Perry gives voice to what such mental freedom has meant for us: "Imagination has always been our gift. That is what makes formulations like 'Black people are naturally good at dancing' so offensive. Years of discipline that turn into improvisation, a mastery of grammar and an idea that turns into a movement that hadn't been precisely like that before—that is imagination, not instinct."

Pelican was a weekly retreat from the usual strictures of schooling—worksheets, homework, and tests were replaced by music, movement, and make-believe. But who decided we could steal away? And from what were we escaping?

Visiting its website, I learned that there are three pathways into the Pelican program—aptitude, achievement, and performance: "The State of South Carolina and the District declares by evaluation and eligibility standards that the gifted child has academic needs that must be met in a differentiated environment." This begs the question: Who thrives in an *undifferentiated* environment?

"The mission of gifted education is to maximize the potential of gifted and talented students by providing programs and services that match the unique characteristics and needs of these students." So, then, is the mission of standard education to *minimize* or hold at bay the potential of most students?

Yes, I think that is precisely what it does, especially if we consider the eugenicist roots of testing and ranking. In the 1920s the College Board commissioned psychologist and eugenicist Carl C. Brigham to develop the Scholastic Aptitude Test (SAT). Brigham, a Princeton alumnus who had recently authored *A Study of American Intelligence* (1923), hailed the superiority of the "Nordic race group" and warned that with the "promiscuous intermingling" of new immigrants, the education system was declining at "an accelerating rate as the racial mixture becomes more and more extensive." Standardized testing has always been predicated on a racist, classist, sexist, and ableist standard.

A world that relies on social inequality to keep its machinery running can only afford for a handful of people to imagine themselves "gifted." Gifted = destined leaders and bosses, visionaries and innovators who have the time and resources to design the future while the masses are trained to sit still, raise their hands, and take instruction.

Doesn't the unbearable hubris and entitlement of many of society's "leaders," whether in industry or politics or even do-gooding professions, stem from us being told all our lives that we are "special"? Or more precisely, of us being *made* special and treated by the law and culture as the chosen ones?

Meanwhile, the majority of "normals" (to borrow a term from the sci-fi film *Gattaca*) are expected to take orders, complete tasks, stand in line, clock in and out . . . punctually, obediently, subserviently. No dancing in the halls, and certainly no daydreaming about a world put together differently.

Mary, Qima, and I were "gifted" alright . . . *gifted* time and space to imagine differently. Not because we *were* different but because we were given a chance *to be* different.

The fact is, "exceptional Negroes" have always been a staple of an apartheid-like educational system that separates the "gifted" from the "normal," and both from the "naughty" or "underachieving." *Sticks and stones will only break my bones, but words can lift or crush me.* For some, the existence of "exceptional Negroes" suggests that the system is not racist. But doesn't such tokenistic inclusion—in which a few individuals are given provisional membership into an other-wise exclusive club—maintain the status quo by making it seem more accessible than it really is?

Without a handful of Black and Brown unicorns in honors classes and gifted programs, we might see more clearly the broader pat-terns of exclusion. We might realize that school tracking perpetuates intraschool segregation, that even when schools are racially diverse, even when they are in the suburban "promised land," they often remain deeply unequal. Indeed, the flip side of hoarding gifted, hon-ors, and Advanced Placement classrooms for predominantly white students is the funneling of Black students into special education and remedial programs, what education researchers describe as de facto racial segregation.

One activity at Pelican that I remember vividly required us to invent new uses for ordinary objects like scissors, rubber bands, and erasers. Years later, I heard a talk by noted educator Sir Ken

Robinson in which he described a study about how researchers measure genius-level "divergent" thinking by assessing students' ability to come up with lots of possible ways of interpreting and answering questions.

In the study, 1,500 kindergarteners were asked questions like "How many uses can you think of for a paper clip?" At that young age, 98 percent of the children scored at "genius level" for divergent thinking. But over the next ten years, this capacity was schooled out of them. "We all have this capacity," insisted Robinson, but "it mostly deteriorates." Yet "deteriorates" makes it seem like a natural process of decay, when really it is a concerted, organized process of squashing an otherwise widespread capacity to think, know, and imagine. As writer and activist adrienne maree brown reminds us, "We are in an imagination battle."

The irony, of course, is that the very place where inventive thinking could be—some would say *should* be—cultivated is where it gets snuffed out. Except, of course, for the lucky few who get pulled out of school and given an opportunity to diverge, experiment, *and* make mistakes.

Otherwise, if you let your imagination run free, you're likely to get into trouble. In 2013, sixteen-year-old Black teenager Kiera Wilmot did a science experiment mixing toilet bowl cleaner and aluminum foil in a water bottle. It caused a small explosion on school grounds, and she was automatically expelled. The Florida assistant state attorney charged her with two felonies filed in adult court. The charges were eventually dropped as part of a diversion program that allows people facing criminal conviction to meet certain service requirements instead.

However, rather than being allowed back into her honors classes,

Kiera had to finish her junior year at an alternative high school—a euphemism, in this case, for a school for "bad" kids. There, Kiera felt intellectually uninspired. As she shared with the American Civil Liberties Union (ACLU): "I'm not getting the challenge that I used to have. I don't have homework. There is no German class, and there is no orchestra." It is doubtful Kiera would have been treated with such contempt were she not Black, and because of the zero-tolerance disciplinary policies that uphold rigid rules and end up alienating and pushing out many young people.

The outsized response to Kiera's science experiment explosion was also fueled by anti-terrorism fervor in the wake of 9/11 and the Boston marathon bombing—her project came just eight days after the latter. Another outcome of these events was an increase in anti-Muslim hatred, which has not waned. According to a 2016 Gallup poll, 38 percent of respondents backed "a new law that would prevent any Muslim from entering the U.S." and 32 percent supported a "special ID" for Muslims, including those who are American citizens. These alarming statistics reflect a long-standing racial imagination that infects social life and periodically erupts into the headlines, as it did in the case of Texas teenager Ahmed Mohamed.

In 2015, Ahmed was interrogated, suspended, and fingerprinted for constructing a clock inside his pencil case. He used a small circuit board, power supply, and digital display, inventively transforming the case. Dismayingly, his teacher and principal suspected the clock of being a bomb. Through the distorting fun-house mirrors of white supremacy and anti-Muslim hatred, he was deemed guilty instead of gifted, threatening instead of talented.

Kiera and Ahmed would eventually meet at the White House

at an Astronomy Night, hosted by President Barack Obama. Yet Kiera's invitation wasn't extended until after online commentary circulated suggesting she should be bestowed the same honor as Ahmed. As Kiera shared, the White House had invited her not so much because of her science project but because of what she called "the arrest and all the hardships. I am a woman of color who was pushed out of school." These hardships reveal that Kiera's path to a White House visit is not the Cinderella story promised to many via the gifted and talented route. Kiera shared at a press conference during her visit to Washington, DC, "To this day, I still get people who harass me about it and call me a terrorist." And she was haunted by a felony arrest, which she was told would take five years to clear from her record.

Unicorn status is a fickle prize that can be revoked as quickly as it is bestowed. Instead of rallying around individual exceptionalism, we need to see the bigger picture and imagine new systems of education that cultivate everyone's creativity and curiosity. So what is there to do?

The most effective means to refute the prevailing ideologies is to do so *collectively*—crafting new stories, images, ways of interacting, and investments in those who have been denigrated and discarded. To think about the collective also means being okay with less focus on exceptionalism and instead giving all students opportunities to stretch their imaginations.

I wrote this book for all the Kieras and Ahmeds of the world, and all those who cross their paths. It is for organizers and artists, students and educators, parents and professors, realists and romantics who are ready to take Toni Morrison's instruction to heart: *Dream a little before you think.*

IN THESE PAGES, I weave together a lifetime of observations about the centrality of imagination in all our lives; lively engagements with people from many different fields who have ruminated on the power of imagination; promiscuous encounters with pop culture and social media where collective imagination is woven and warped; and practical guidance on how we can exercise our imaginations.

I draw upon over a decade of teaching that aims to build students' powers of speculation with projects that involve imagining tools, toolkits, and worlds that break with current social hierarchies. In the process, we will confront the little voice in our head whose job it has been to police our own imaginations: A world without prisons? *Ridiculous.* Schools that foster the genius of every child? *Impossible.* Work that doesn't grind us to the bone? *Naive.* A society where everyone has food, shelter, *love*? *In your dreams.* Exactly.

We need to give the voice of the cynical, skeptical grouch that patrols the borders of our imagination a rest. After all, "Dangerous limits have been placed on the very possibility of imagining alternatives," insists scholar and activist Angela Y. Davis. "These ideological limits have to be contested. We have to begin to think in different ways. Our future is at stake." Imagination is a field of struggle, not an ephemeral afterthought that we have the luxury to dismiss or romanticize.

Imagination: A Manifesto is a proposal for exorcising our mental and social structures from the tyranny of dominant imaginaries. It is a field guide for seeding an imagination grounded in solidarity, in which our underlying interdependence as a species and with the rest of the planet is reflected back at us in our institutions and social relationships.

Look around: humanity is in the eye of multiple storms. Will we continue shutting off the power of the masses so that a minority of people can stay warm, or will we build the necessary infrastructure so that everyone can thrive? Like author Arundhati Roy, I believe "another world is not only possible, she is on her way. . . . On a quiet day, if I listen very carefully, I can hear her breathing."

If I didn't define myself for myself,
I would be crunched into other people's fantasies for me
and eaten alive.

—Audre Lorde

CHAPTER ONE

WHOSE IMAGINATION?

———

WHEN MY KIDS were little, I waged a cold war against organized sports. It started when my older son received a basketball-themed birthday card. It intensified when my younger one was gifted a lovingly sewn quilt adorned with images of footballs, baseballs, and soccer balls. I knew I had a problem when, instead of cheering on the sidelines at one of their games, I sat Scrooge-like in the car. But things really grew absurd when, at a middle-school basketball game, I found myself (a prolific point guard in high school) quietly cheering anytime my kid, the only Black player on the team, shot air balls, got penalties for traveling, and missed elegant passes from teammates.

It wasn't that I was rooting against my son, or even that I was against sports writ large. It was more that I was opposed to the fantasies swirling around the Black Athlete. Brawn over brain, muscle over mind, physical prowess over all other types of ingenuity. Yes, I know, these are false binaries. No one fits neatly within these either/or propositions. But still, I felt embattled against organized sports as it looms over American childhoods and vexed by the flattened figure of the Black Athlete as it looms over athletics. At every turn I found myself sparring with the stereotype that "Black people are good at sports" and attempting to slay the eugenic belief in "natural" ability. I wanted so badly to protect my sons from being conscripted into this culturally assigned role where their identities would revolve around their ability to run, jump, kick, and catch.

When I think back on it, I'm tempted to chalk it up to young mama zeal. How else to explain the way I read entire histories of race and objectification into a simple sports-themed birthday card? But then I remember, even supposedly positive stereotypes—"Asians are smart," "Latinos are passionate," "Indigenous peoples are spiritual," "Black folks can dance"—have a sinister underside. If you are innately gifted at something, doesn't that imply you don't have to work as hard at it to excel? If you are genetically predisposed toward one thing, doesn't that mean you could be inherently deficient in another?

Sociologist Patricia Hill Collins describes stereotypes as "controlling images," because they box us in no matter their valence, negative or positive. The irony is that even when we try to *avoid* falling into a stereotype (like I was) they are controlling us.

Beyond the stereotyping effect, what continues to disturb me about the Black Athlete is the white entitlement that ensnares this celebrated figure. I think of NFL quarterback Colin Kaepernick, who, in 2016, first took a knee during the national anthem to bring attention to police brutality, and the white audiences who demanded he "shut up and play," while the team owners blacklisted him from the league because "he was bad for business."

I think of gymnastics champion Simone Biles, who, in 2021, decided to withdraw from the Olympics finals after experiencing the "twisties" (a frightening experience when gymnasts lose control of their bodies in the air), and the public blowback she received, being called a "selfish sociopath" and a "shame to the country."

I think of Kylian Mbappé, who, in 2022, led the French national soccer team to second place in the World Cup, and how he and his teammate Kingsley Coman were the targets of racist abuse online following the last match, despite Mbappé having performed the extraordinary feat of scoring two back-to-back goals within minutes to tie with Argentina.

I think, too, of the countless retired Black football players who suffer from dementia but who, until 2021, were denied settlement awards from the NFL's concussion fund because they were presumed to have lower baseline cognitive function than their white counterparts simply because they were Black.

One after another "crunched into other people's fantasies and eaten alive."

Picture it: stadiums full of white fans who cheer on the Black Athlete—touchdowns, home runs, slam dunks—but who have no Black friends, avoid hiring Black employees, protest Black history in their children's schools. They are happy to be entertained by panting Black bodies, but they look away from the brutality meted out to breathless Black *people* off the field.

I think of seventeen-year-old Trayvon Martin, who, in 2012, was making a snack run when he was shot dead by George Zimmerman in a Florida gated community at the very moment when millions of Americans were rooting for their favorite (mostly Black) players during the NBA All-Star Game. A deadly hypocrisy, as I see it, when it comes to how Blackness is selectively celebrated (and contained) within the white imagination.

"Know-your-place aggression" is what scholar Koritha Mitchell calls it when the success of marginalized groups is met with backlash. This certainly applies to Serena Williams and the unrelenting disdain that has greeted her lifetime of achievements. In other cases, like that of Biles and tennis champion Naomi Osaka, Black athletes are expected to keep performing no matter the cost to their own well-being. "Don't you dare step out of bounds" is the warning. Or, like with Kaepernick, white aggression is directed at those whose achievements are hailed on the field, but who are deemed a menace when they dare exercise agency in other contexts, especially if they threaten America's "idealized representation of itself" as the Land of the Free, Home of the Brave.

These are but a sampling of high-profile instances of adulation-turned-antipathy. Meanwhile, what some call the "college sports industrial complex" remains a billion-dollar industry fueled by Black talent—"TV deals, new stadiums, corporate sponsorships and ballooning salaries for everyone—except the players." Civil rights historian Taylor Branch has uncovered the deep hypocrisy and false benevolence of a college sports industry that romanticizes "amateurism" and celebrates "free education" for players, many of whom still cannot afford a movie ticket or a bus ride home. But Black athletes are rising up, demanding a say in the governance of their sport, calling for fair compensation, threatening to boycott, and filing class-action lawsuits against the National Collegiate Athletic Association.

As a young mom seeking to cultivate confidence and courage in my children, not only in the narrow domain of sports but as they move freely and fully through the world, I struggled against the allure of the Black Athlete. And it is quite possible that my militancy stems from suspicions that my own father's stroke and early death are linked to his days as a college football player.

The irony is that, as young adults, one of my sons walked on as an NCAA Division 1 rower (with no prior experience) and the other was voted captain of his college rugby team. *Le sigh, I tried.* Interesting that they gravitated toward activities that, in the U.S., do not have a large fanbase and have very little Black representation. The better, perhaps, to experience the highs, lows, and rush of sport without the cheering or jeering of white crowds at their necks.

THE POINT REMAINS: Games are serious business. They reflect and reinforce broader social patterns of power and inequality. Take the game Monopoly, which has sold over 250 million units since Parker Brothers began mass producing it in 1935. Most people don't know that the precursor to Monopoly was the Landlord's Game, created by feminist anti-monopolist Elizabeth Magie. Magie, like so many others at the time, was inspired by economist Henry George's 1879 best-seller, *Progress and Poverty*. She decided to create a game to demonstrate the evils of monopoly, inviting players to reject the impoverishment and displacement upon which gross concentrations of wealth depend. She applied for a patent in 1903, and three decades later, Parker Brothers would pay her only $500 for the rights.

Although Magie intended players to experience the game as a fantasy that eats us alive, monopolizing power and resources ends up, for many of us, being the object of desire, not disdain. Those of us trapped inside the Capitalist Dream are taught to identify with the winner and look down on the losers. "Aporophobia" is what philosopher Adela Cortina calls the fear, hatred, and rejection directed at poor people. The question is, should we try to change the rules to allow for more winners? Or is it possible to subvert the game, maybe even stop playing, and imagine a social and economic system that doesn't immiserate the masses to enrich the few?

Take the board game Co-opoly, launched in 2011, which simulates what it is like to be employed in a worker cooperative in which we either "all win or all lose." Rather than warn us of the evils of capitalist exploitation, as Magie had hoped to do with her 1903 invention, the creators of Co-opoly take it a step further by introducing players to the joy and pleasure of cooperative economics. This is a good reminder that we shouldn't shine a light only on the deadly imaginations and social orders that are killing us but experiment and play with new prescriptions, visions, and forms of social organization.

I LIKE HOW CULTURAL HISTORIAN Thomas Berry put it when he said "We are in between stories." The Old Stories, as I see them, include those scripted by colonialism, capitalism, ableism, white supremacy, nationalism, and cis-heteropatriarchy. All require us to believe in the inherent, God-given superiority of some groups over others. They include master narratives like:

The Doctrine of Discovery—a principle of international law originating from a papal decree by the Catholic Church in 1493, which gave Christian nations license to seize and colonize any land they found occupied by non-Christians, including present-day North, Central, and South America, and to convert and enslave the millions of people already living there;

Manifest Destiny—a phrase coined in 1845 to describe the widespread belief that white settlers were destined by God to colonize the Americas, thereby justifying the forced removal of Indigenous peoples from their lands;

Survival of the Fittest—a concept devised by philosopher Herbert Spencer in 1864 to describe the "preservation of favored races [i.e., whites] in the struggle for life," which helped justify racial hierarchies as a natural byproduct of cutthroat competition between those who are strong and those who are weak. Strength, not in terms of muscular strength, but intellectual, moral, and cultural fitness so that, as sociologist Rina Bliss explains, those from what were deemed weaker races "had to be prevented from passing on their genes."

Talk about deadly stories of entitlement and domination. These Old Stories continue to infect our collective imagination, distorting how we see and value different groups, cultures, and worldviews. They even warp our conception of "human nature"—selfish, not altruistic; competitive, not cooperative; hardwired, not adaptable. They presuppose a fixed genetic or cultural predisposition that ignores the plasticity of our brains and the malleability of our social relations.

"But, Dr. Benjamin, the racial conflicts you describe today go back centuries; the suspicions we have for different groups are in our DNA!" Oh, how many times have I heard a variant of this view, usually after one of my talks, where the retreat into genetic and historical absolutes implies there is no use trying to write new stories. But I cannot abide that kind of intellectual fatalism, nor can most people who experience the deadly consequence of those Old Stories.

If we are "between stories," as Berry suggests, then we can work to discard the lies we have inherited that glorify hierarchy, monopoly, and greed. If we are to create a world in which the strong and the weak survive, a world in which "weakness" itself is imagined differently, then we must write new stories that engender solidarity, mutuality, and shared prosperity. Berry outlines four pillars that maintain those outmoded stories: religions, governments, corporations, and universities. Given the centrality of religion in animating the master narratives I've sketched above, the next chapter will focus on the last three pillars, broadening universities to include schooling writ large and reflecting on what new, liberating stories we could and should write.

But lest we assume a simplified choice between Old Stories and new ones, in reality, new-ish stories abound. These far-out tales of utopian futures come packaged in the dazzlingly white and sterile imaginations of tech titans and billionaire entrepreneurs. Their fantastic fables transport us into visions of artificially enhanced post-humans numbering in the trillions who "live rich and happy lives" in their virtual habitats. Listen carefully and you'll hear how these new-ish stories gloss over an unsavory subtext: That the rich, powerful, and pedigreed know what is best for all. And what *is* best? To avoid "existential risk" at all costs. *X-risk*, as insiders call it, is anything that would endanger a future "multi-galactic civilization" populated by digital people—"post-humans in vast computer simulations spread throughout the universe." Too bizarre to be taken seriously? Perhaps. But just imagine all the ruinous possibilities as the self-appointed stewards of humanity work to colonize the future.

Drawing on firsthand encounters with AI-evangelists-turned-doomers, Ethiopian-born computer scientist Timnit Gebru points out the hypocrisy: "They don't ever want to talk about real issues they might be implicated in, like racism, sexism, or imperialism. They want to talk about grand visions of saving humanity . . . wanting to feel like a savior and not wanting to feel like a problem."

Guided by the gospels of "radical longtermism" and "effective altruism" (EA), these newfangled storytellers are devoted to the flourishing of imaginary future people rather than the well-being of the masses right here, right now. Longtermist Nick Beckstead did us all a service by saying the quiet part out loud:

Saving lives in poor countries may have significantly smaller ripple effects than saving and improving lives in rich countries. Why? Richer countries have substantially more innovation, and their workers are much more economically productive.

The tech elite, in this vision, are more valuable than the rest of us. Most altruism, EA adherents argue, is ineffective because it focuses on the wrong ends.

As philosopher and historian Émile P. Torres warns, "Over and over again throughout history, the combination of these two ingredients—utopianism and the belief that ends justify the means—has been disastrous. . . . *All the ingredients* needed to 'justify' atrocities are present in the longtermist ideology—indeed, they lie at its *very core*." Even climate change is not high on the list of priorities, so long as at least some people survive to ensure the eventual creation of digital descendants. "So let's not get too worked up about it: There are bigger fish to fry," implies longtermist John Halstead.

When we tune in carefully, we hear longtermism echoing a eugenics calculus that some believe we have left in the dustbins of history: the weak must be sacrificed so the strong survive. In this new era, strength is associated not with mere intelligence with but superintelligence, sole province of those who "use advanced technologies to radically enhance themselves."

In early January 2023, Nick Bostrom, head of Oxford's Future of Humanity Institute, defended himself against racist remarks he made on a Listserve in the 1990s. Whether you believe him or not, or whether you think it matters that Bostrom did or does hold these racist judgments, the fact remains: those who are shaping the "future of humanity," as his institute purports to do, are gathered from a very small sliver of humanity, and their views—racist, utopian, both, and—are currently occupying the imaginative space to which the rest of us have a right. The problem goes beyond one individual to longtermism itself, which centers wealthy tech innovators—mostly white and male—as those who should survive into the future because they are the best of the human race.

For some of the most outspoken proponents of longtermism, humanity as we now know it, flesh-and-blood *Homo sapiens*, is old-school. These advocates are enamored by the prospect of digital descendants who, in the deep future, they believe will be (should be?) granted the same moral standing as you and me. In their new-ish stories, the most important task we face is ensuring the "longterm potential" of imaginary future people rather than working to alleviate human suffering in the here and now—those pesky "feel-good projects" like eliminating poverty, addressing climate change, and preventing catastrophic wars. All of us—teachers, students, policymakers, journalists, artists, businesspeople, gig workers, and all those pushed to the margins—should take this warped imagination seriously.

Indeed, if there's one thing I hope you take away from reading this book, it is that you will commit to keeping your critical antennae tuned in to the nightmarish fantasies of post-human proselytizers, among them many Silicon Valley elite and superintelligentsia, who believe the best thing they can do for humanity is "get filthy rich, for charity's sake." Why? Because those who monopolize resources monopolize imagination.

As Torres cautions, longtermism is not only fueling massive investment in AI as a necessary step toward the evolution of trans-humans, what some might still consider fringe concerns, but it is snaking its way into the global mainstream. Torres points to a UN Dispatch article stating that "the foreign policy community in general and the United Nations in particular are beginning to embrace longtermism." If politicians and policymakers accept the eugenics calculus of this movement as inevitable and necessary, there is no telling what suffering they will justify on the road to longterm bliss.

But even if the threatening nature of this new-ish imagination doesn't yet feel urgent to you, I at least hope your critical facul-ties are tingling. Now you can readily tune in to the hollow ethi-cal commitments of these so-called visionaries, and you can counsel your children and grandchildren, so that they will be attentive to the deceitful machinations of those who fancy themselves the self-appointed stewards of humanity. As each new generation expands their imagination, let them also develop a keener ability to detect bullshit. Each of us can foster the kind of discernment that tells the difference between New Stories of collective well-being and Faux Fables deciding our collective fate.

One way to tell if your vision of the future is new or just new-ish is whether it seriously aims to alleviate the injustice and suffering of the present. The choice is not between effective and ineffective altruism, but between solidarity and indifference when it comes to flesh-and-blood people whom those planning looooong-term would rather we abandon. If our imagination turns its back on the experiences and insights of those buried under the weight of brutal social structures in the here and now, then it can only ever be -ish.

In *Freedom Dreams: The Black Radical Imagination*, Robin D. G. Kelley opens with a moving tribute to his mother—a woman who, though raising her children under harsh social and economic conditions, enjoined them to "see the poetic and prophetic" in the richness of everyday life, and to believe that "the map to a new world is in the imagination." Kelley is a cartographer of liberation, mapping freedom dreams of all kinds—from Maroon societies of the formerly enslaved to Black nationalists, communists, surrealists, and feminists. He explores how renegade Black intellectuals, artists, and activists across all these movements "imagined life after the revolution."

For me, there is no way to read Kelley and remain mired in a "culture of cynicism" or retain the solemn and detached posture of a supposedly "serious" academic. The stakes are too high and the stubborn hopefulness of those struggling to re-create this gloomy world too contagious to resign myself to dour pessimism. Alongside a clear-headed pragmatism, *Freedom Dreams* invites us to witness and create *poetic knowledge*—"*that* imagination, that effort to see the future in the present."

Radical imagination, then, isn't counter to doing the work of changing our material conditions and improving our quality of life.

Rather, radical imagination can inspire us to push beyond the constraints of what we think, and are told, is politically possible. While I am most concerned with how and what we dream collectively, there are lessons we can learn from how individuals, like Kelley's mother, strive to protect their imaginations in the day-to-day work of fashioning their lives within oppressive systems.

You can see this power of imagination at work in my favorite scene from *Being Serena*, the HBO Max docuseries about tennis champion Serena Williams. Serena is seven or eight years old, practicing with her father, Richard Williams, by her side. As she runs back and forth on a public court in their Compton neighborhood, clad in a fuchsia tennis skirt and oversized white collared shirt, with short braided hair, Richard calls out, "This is you at the US Open . . . *Boom!*"

I am always struck that Richard doesn't say, "Imagine one day you're playing at the US Open." Instead, his choice of words places Serena on that world stage in the here and now. *This is you at the US Open.* In his mind (and hers, perhaps) she is already there. The rush of excitement, the fierce competition, the intense scrutiny of her every move, and the cheering crowds flood her imagination, all before she even hits double digits in age. *Boom!* Richard's words transport Serena, who started playing at the tender age of three. His precise wording, *This is you*, works like a portal, beaming Serena into a future where she is a world champion. Or so it seems from the exquisite editing of the documentary.

In reality, King Richard's words did not magically conjure Serena's stardom, though the skillful juxtaposition of past and present footage makes Serena's story appear predestined. Rather, it was the thousands of hours practicing, saving money, and working toward a goal as a family that propelled Serena and her sister, Venus, forward. Words and affirmations alone do not a future make. It was the hustling day in and out to raise the cold, hard cash to pay for all that was required in an expensive sport, while convincing the white establishment that Venus and Serena had what it took to be great.

Zach Baylin, scriptwriter of *King Richard*, a movie based on Richard Williams's training of Serena and Venus, observed Richard's brilliance: "He knew that without the resources, he was going to have to build up this *aura and myth* around them to get people to invest in [Venus and Serena]." He had to conjure good stories, ones that shimmered with the girls' potential and predestination. In his pitch to Vic Braden, the most famous tennis instructor at the time, Richard played a homemade highlights reel of the girls playing tennis and answering questions, all part of their "media training," he told Braden.

But Braden wasn't convinced, telling Richard, "It's like asking someone to believe you've got the next two Mozarts in your house." Undeterred, Richard crashed a practice session with tennis champs John McEnroe and Pete Sampras, handing McEnroe a homemade brochure and saying that his (then unknown) daughters would "sign it for you later."

Finally, after dozens of rejections, Richard convinced renowned coach Rick Macci to take on the girls, and Macci gushed, "I think you may have the next Michael Jordan on your hands." But Richard corrected him, "Oh, no, brotherman, I gots me the next two," an actual exchange that got depicted on the big screen.

Those forecasts, it turns out, were directed not only to the outside world but also to Venus and Serena. "You gonna be the best there ever was. You gonna be the greatest of all time," he once told Serena in real life. Moving from the dramatized film to documentary footage of the Williams family, by the time an interviewer asked the young player whom she looked forward to playing on an upcoming tour, Serena's self-regard shone bright: "Well, I'd like other people to want to play like me."

Together, Richard Williams and Oracene Price sought to cultivate *and* protect their children's imaginations. As Venus and Serena's elder sister Isha Price commented, "The weirdest thing to us was that we couldn't watch *The Cosby Show*. . . . Daddy said, Bill Cosby was already rich. Why sit around and watch him when we need to be coming up with our plan?" Richard, then, was not a storyteller as much as he was a story*maker. Why be drawn into someone else's fictional world when you could be living out dreams of your own?* His mythmaking went hand in hand with meticulous planning; his seventy-eight-page blueprint for transforming his daughters into tennis stars is itself a thing of legend. But he was also adamant that his daughters not be defined strictly as Black Athletes, encouraging them to learn multiple languages and pursue outside interests, like fashion and business, even though this caused the tennis establishment to question their dedication.

From the Williams family we learn that *making a way outta no way* cannot be reduced to feel-good self-help affirmations or mind-over-matter platitudes. That said, for Black feminist scholar Brittney Cooper, "Sometimes for us [Black women], mind over matter really does become the only way that we have going for us." Cooper's mom taught her "that dreaming is at the core of politics. If things are going to get better, Black women have to stay invested in the project of dreaming." The kind of tenacity it takes to turn a blueprint into reality can look like a ridiculous flight of fancy to someone standing outside one's dream. Indeed, the white tennis establishment and media routinely cast Richard Williams as "crazy" and "bombastic" as he fiercely ensured they did not contaminate his daughters' dreams with doubts and prejudice.

Finally, it was not the power of imagination alone but a confluence of factors, including the Williams family's determination against all odds, the daughters' ability and work, and Richard and Oracene's initial coaching, that ensured theirs was not another *dream deferred*. So, too, when we work to cultivate a collective vision for transforming the world, we must be careful not to fetishize imagination as somehow operating magically and independently from other powerful ingredients, like strategizing and organizing, to make our vision a reality.

Indeed, there's a danger that in carving out space to take imagination seriously in these pages, I leave you with the impression that we can simply imagine ourselves out of the death-making machinery humming in the background of our schools, jobs, and neighborhoods. Deadly eugenic imaginaries animate political regimes and bureaucratic structures, without which it would be impossible to materialize the noxious harms that flood our news feeds and our lives.

Yet, in focusing only on the material basis of harm—environmental hazards, brutal police officers, and discriminatory employment algorithms, to name a few—we may overlook the ideas and ideologies that continue to give rise to those harms again and again. If, as Kelley laments, "There are very few contemporary political spaces where the energies of love and imagination are understood and respected as powerful social forces," then our aim here is to carve out those spaces by *all* means possible.

because white men can't
police their imagination
black men are dying
—Claudia Rankine

CHAPTER TWO

IMAGINING OURSELVES

———

M OST OF US tend to associate "imagination" with a joyful awakening of the mind—which it *can* be. But look closer, and you'll see that imagination is not a wholesale good. It is easy to lose sight of the array of oppressive imaginaries that more casually govern our lives. The American Dream. The Chinese Dream. The Great British Dream. The Indian Dream. All around us we see how nationalist imaginaries conscript us into their provincial projects that are steeped in various brands of chauvinism. Nationalism produces and relies upon "imagined communities" whose allure is exceptionalism, righteousness, and superiority.

Patriotism requires that we accept the superstition of our specialness, parrot the propaganda of our destiny, and repeat the lie of our chosenness. But what if we told the truth? What if, like poet Derek Walcott, we considered that "I had no nation now but the imagination." What if we looked to the stars and reckoned with our planetary interconnectedness and the deadly fault lines that continue to tear us apart?

"The Eagle has landed! Man on the moon." In the documentary

Summer of Soul, directed by the musical artist Ahmir "Questlove" Thompson, Thompson overlays the original footage from the July 16, 1969, moon landing with the Staple Singers crooning the lyric "One of these days, there'll be a man on the moon." Short interview clips follow, of white Americans around the country awestruck and gushing:

> *"It's a great thing for this country."*
> *"It's a great technological achievement."*
> *"I felt the world got closer today."*

But the moon landing is not the focus of the documentary. Instead, set against that scientific feat, another awesome event of that summer, the weeks-long Harlem Cultural Festival, is the center of attention. "Black Woodstock," as many people called it, brought together the most notable Black singers and bands of the time, from Nina Simone to Stevie Wonder, Mahalia Jackson, and more.

"There are forty thousand, perhaps fifty thousand people at Mount Morris Park in Harlem," observes a TV news reporter as images from the festival flash across the screen, "but they are not here watching the moon landing. They are here at the Soul Festival . . . and, for many of them, *this* is far more relevant than the mission of Apollo 11."

"What's your feeling now that the astronauts have landed safely on the moon?" the reporter asks members of the jam-packed audience.

"I think it's very important," says one man, "but I don't think it's any more relevant than the Harlem Cultural Festival here. I think it's equal."

"As far as science goes and everybody that's involved with the moon landing and astronauts, it's beautiful, you know," says another. "Like me, I couldn't care less. The cash they wasted, as far as I'm concerned, in getting to the moon could've been used to feed poor Black people in Harlem and all over this country. Never mind the moon, let's get some of that cash in Harlem."

Even on the main stage, artists and comedians poke fun at the landing. When ventriloquist act Willie Tyler and Lester say that instead of planting a flag on the moon, they would have rather planted a sign saying, "For Sale . . . *Cheap!*" the crowd bursts into knowing laughter and applause. The subtext: this is white America's dream, not theirs.

The dissonance of that moment in 1969 must have inspired Amiri Baraka's poetic essay, "Technology and Ethos," written that same year:

> Nothing *has* to look or function the way it does. The West man's freedom, unscientifically got at the expense of the rest of the world's people, has allowed him to xpand his mind—spread his sensibility wherever it *cd* go, & so *shaped* the world, & its powerful artifact-engines.

In the film's poignant juxtapositions, we witness a clash of imaginations—a governing white imagination captivated by the utopian possibilities of space travel, and a Black social imagination demanding attention to the dystopias right under our noses.

CAPITALISM, TOO, WARPS our vision. Fast-forward some fifty years from the moon landing: today we witness billionaires Elon Musk, Jeff Bezos, and Richard Branson in an interplanetary race of their own. They are peddling "the idea that space represents a public hope, all the while reaping big private profits," notes scholar Alina Utrata. For all the accolades showered upon these men as visionary entrepreneurs, "their celestial utopias stand out for their lack of political creativity and awareness."

When Musk's spaceflight company, SpaceX, which aims to eventually send a manned crew to Mars, moved to Texas, people and wildlife were pushed out because rocket activity made the surrounding area unsafe. At the same time that Jeff Bezos took a four-minute, $5.5-billion trip on a lunar lander developed by his company Blue Origin, Amazon warehouse workers continued racing against the clock to make ends meet.

As one observer mused: "With Bezos in space, there's never been a better time for Amazon workers to finally go take a bathroom break." And in response to Bezos thanking Amazon employees and customers for his trip "because you guys paid for all of this," Congresswoman Alexandria Ocasio-Cortez tweeted, "Yes, Amazon workers did pay for this—with lower wages, union busting, a frenzied and inhumane workplace, and delivery drivers not having health insurance during a pandemic. And Amazon customers are paying for it with Amazon abusing their market power to hurt small business."

Scientist and activist Vandana Shiva calls out plans for space colonization as based in "the illusory idea of linear human progress," which fails to recognize that "this is our home, the only one we have, and that the crisis we find ourselves in is, in fact, a consequence of the colonisation of the earth, of diverse cultures, and of the absence of accountability for the destruction caused by colonisation." Or, as one Twitter observer put it, "You can't buy your way out of the death of the biosphere."

In addition to space exploration, billionaires are looking to the sea for their next ventures. Peter Thiel (cofounder of PayPal and founder of the surveillance company Palantir) and libertarian Patri Friedman (former Google engineer and grandson of greed-is-good economist Milton Friedman) have teamed up to create organizations like the Seasteading Institute to develop floating ocean platforms that house "permanent, autonomous ocean communities, enabling innovations with new political and social systems," or political startups. As Utrata reports, "Like the space colonizers, seasteaders imagine that human engineering will be able to create new, virgin territories—in the sea or stars—which will provide the 'space' to solve political problems." These "start-up nations" represent Silicon Valley elites' vision to once and for all "cede from the state, both territorially and politically" and be completely free from the regulatory hold of all existing governments. Talk about a wildly insular imagination.

And yet, as I will elaborate later in the book, there are already aquatic communities around the world that employ ancient technologies to construct floating islands—from the Maʻdan in the southern wetlands of Iraq to the Uros who live on the waters of Lake Titicaca in Peru—which our modern mythos views as "primitive" rather than innovative.

Indeed, disregard for "premodern" peoples and their inventions is precisely why we face a planetary crisis, and why a handful of tech bros are betting on salvation in the stars and seas . . . or in a galaxy millions, even billions of years into the future where our digital descendants have no need for clean water or air. But why *on earth* would we believe that a colonizing impulse would magically lead to universal prosperity this time around?

Perhaps the point is, we don't need to believe if we are not even privy to the machinations of the uber-rich, those fabricating islands, settling solar systems, and gestating transhumans who will suckle upon their bankrupt philosophies. More on that in just a bit, but first, what clouds our powers of perception?

There exists a multibillion-dollar Soft Power (Dream) Industry, which is in the business of crafting and selling powerful myths that lull us into various states of zombielike consumerism—swiping, subscribing, and submitting to its narrow vision of belonging. This Capitalist Dream skips along to the beat of the New York Stock Exchange's trading-floor bells, inviting us to dance along to the notification pings of our latest Amazon Prime delivery. As historian Robin D. G. Kelley asks, "Even if we could gather together our dreams of a new world, how do we figure them out in a culture dominated by the marketplace?"

As far back as 1935, renowned scholar and activist W. E. B. Du Bois observed: "Two theories of the future of America clashed and blended just after the Civil War: the one was abolition-democracy based on freedom, intelligence, and power for all men; the other was industry for private profit directed by an autocracy determined at any price to amass wealth and power." Doesn't this speak to the fact that theories are never *merely* theoretical? And that theories, ideas, and imaginaries can be enacted toward building or breaking society? Today, the planet is ensnared within that second theory Du Bois warned of, with individuals, communities, and the earth itself suffering as a result. But this also means that *alternative* theories, ideas, and imaginaries are vital to our planetary and multispecies survival.

IMAGINE FOR A MOMENT: You are transported to a near future in which the human population is plagued by the spread of mass insomnia, and where many eventually die of sleeplessness. This is the premise of Karen Russell's novella *Sleep Donation*, in which a private company, Slumber Corps, seeks to profit from the crisis by soliciting "sleep donations," and harvesting dreams to keep people alive.

The main protagonist is Trish Edgewater. As a highly skilled sleep-donor recruiter, she uses her insomniac sister's death to inspire donors to give up the goods. Trish reflects,

> America's great talent, I think, is to generate desires that would never have occurred, natively, to a body like mine, and to make those desires so painfully real that money becomes a fiction, an imaginary means to some concrete end.

At one point, an anonymous donor "infects" the Sleep Bank with a nightmare that turns lethal. The story invites us to consider the relationship between restiveness and repose, and how the ease of a small stratum of the global population is predicated on extracting wealth, health, and *rest* from the masses. It holds a mirror up to the overstimulated, sleep-deprived societies of our present day.

The story makes me think of my birthplace, India, where an estimated 3.1 million people work in call centers that are scheduled to accommodate international customers; the daylight hours of the callers dictate the sleep patterns of the night-shift workers. As a result, *shift work disorder* is on the rise, which includes potential risks like "cardiovascular disease, metabolic disorders, cancer, and cognitive impairment"—a real-life form of sleep extraction that can lead to early death. This is a *eugenic* relationship through which the ease and well-being of one group is tied to the immiseration and potential elimination of another.

Most importantly, *Sleep Donation* invites us to consider dreaming as a social practice: What does it mean to actively produce, donate, transfuse, or even contaminate dreams? How do we know if we are dreaming our own *or* others' transplanted dreams?

"To be aware of . . . the market of competing dreams is quite important, when we think about what kind of a new story . . . we should be able to tell," says Indra Adnan, of the political platform Alternative UK. Indeed, we must urgently transition from our current provincial, chauvinistic, and hierarchical nightmare to a planetary vision of human connection, solidarity, and shared prosperity.

SCHOOLS ARE PLACES where the next generation either comes alive with possibility or is crushed by the weight of odds stacked against them. The very place where our imaginations should be fostered is where that potential is routinely smothered. Remember Kiera and Ahmed? These are more obvious attempts at "spirit murder," to borrow legal scholar Patricia J. Williams's term. More recently, twenty-year-old Leilla Hamoud, a student at Winston-Salem State University, a historically Black institution, was handcuffed and dragged out of class by campus police after an argument over an assignment with her white Latinx professor, Cynthia Villagomez, showing that even spaces designed for Black and other marginalized people can be infected by a carceral imagination, one that presents punishment as a reasonable response to all manner of conflict and crisis.

Beyond these individual cases, the widespread practice of enacting zero-tolerance disciplinary policies, segregating students by ability, and making funding decisions that cut art and music classes or that shorten recess all contribute to stifling school environments. School as a site of spirit murder has a long history. Established by the U.S. and Canadian governments in the 1800s, Indian residential schools ripped children from their families and communities, banned their languages and religions, shaved their heads, and changed their names. The goal was to "erase and replace," killing the Indian while "saving the man," and students were regularly beaten and killed while in forced submission to cultural genocide under the guise of education.

Today, the whiteness of the curriculum in many schools continues to perpetuate, albeit more subtly and usually without the threat of physical harm, an ongoing campaign of erasure that arrests the creativity and ingenuity of young people. It not only stunts the potential of those from marginalized groups but also narrows the worldviews of those deemed "privileged."

Recall education scholar Rudine Sims Bishop's metaphor of books as mirrors and windows. While mirrors allow us to see ourselves, windows allow us to see the worlds of others. The whiteness of the curriculum means that marginalized students cannot see themselves reflected back, or when they do, the image is "distorted, negative, or laughable." But those who see themselves everywhere, a kind of structural narcissism, experience an inflated and unimpeachable sense of their own importance and rightness, becoming "victims of their own brainwashing." In contrast, according to writer James Baldwin,

> The American Negro has the great advantage of having never believed the collection of myths to which white Americans cling: that their ancestors were all freedom-loving heroes, that they were born in the greatest country the world has ever seen.

The recent war against "critical race theory" (CRT) in the United States is really a war against anything that undermines the collection of myths to which Baldwin referred. This is why #BanCRT proponents have encouraged (white) parents to "stay on the lookout" for words like *diversity*, *anti-racism*, *identity*, and *social construct*, among others, in their children's classes. Whether they actively enlist or decline to resist, those parents who support this war against words are blacking out the windows of their children's imaginations. Both parent and child find themselves trapped, their images distorted by white supremacy's pathetic hysterics.

For young people of all backgrounds, schooling in the U.S. is a pressure-cooker of stressors, including bullying and other mental health triggers. Is it any wonder that for the past forty years researchers have documented a correlation between youth suicide and the school calendar, with the highest rates when school is in session and the lowest during the summer months? More revealing still, teen suicides plummeted in March 2020, just as the Covid-19 lockdown began, the first time a drop has been observed during the spring since data was first collected in 1980. But the drop was short-lived. When students returned to in-person instruction, teen suicides increased again by 12 to 18 percent. Why is it that the very place that should awaken our potential contributes to depression and death?

Lest we forget, designing cruel, oppressive structures involves imagination too. Consider the ongoing threats to our shared social imagination from the imposition of a techno-utopian, eugenic imagination that seeks to colonize all ways of thinking and being in the world. Whether we are talking about gene editing for healthcare, predictive policing for public safety, or algorithmic risk scoring for education, tech fixes abound—classifying, ranking, and forecasting our futures.

Imagination, then, does not just animate sci-fi-inspired scientific endeavors or explicitly creative pursuits like Broadway musicals, viral TikTok dances, and Jean-Michel Basquiat's paintings. Imagination is also embedded in the more mundane things that govern our lives, like money, laws, and grades.

Professor of collective intelligence, public policy, and social innovation Geoff Mulgan warns that humanity faces an *imaginary crisis*, or "the deteriorating state of our shared social imagination." Perhaps, though, it is not naturally deteriorating but actively *arrested*, given the deep social fault lines and deadly inequalities that impact not only our everyday lives but our ability to imagine something different.

Earlier in my career, I researched the social dimensions of biotechnology, and one of the things I regularly observed was how proponents of cutting-edge advancements in medicine did not limit their aspirations to what was "practical." As one journalist reporting on the $3 billion California Stem Cell Initiative put it, "Imagine cardiac cells, beating in a petri dish, being used to form human tissue that might be used to replace damaged heart muscle." Imagine, indeed.

Scientific inquiry, it turns out, is situated as much in the realm of imagination as it is in the realm of reason. This led me to wonder: Why can we imagine growing heart cells from scratch in a lab, but not growing empathy for other human beings in our everyday lives, and even more so in our institutions? Even well-resourced schools where young people are encouraged to dream big fall short when it comes to cultivating moral imagination.

Rather than serving as engines of inequality, could we imagine schools that incubate a better world in the minds and hearts of young people? For many, the idea that we can defy politics as usual and channel human ingenuity toward more egalitarian forms of social organization is utterly far-fetched! Instead, our collective imagination tends to shrink when confronted with entrenched inequality and injustice, when what we need is to pour just as much investment and ingenuity into transforming our social reality as we do our material reality. This is what I have in mind when I say our classrooms could be laboratories for social change, incubators for seeding a solidaristic imagination.

But to romanticize imagination as inherently ethical and always socially liberating, as in the Kingian refrain "I have a dream . . . ," misses how imagination is the invisible substructure, the narrative code, that shapes our material and digital worlds. Simply put, imagination is not a wholesale "good." After all, the AR-15 semiautomatic weapon, which a gunman used to kill nineteen schoolchildren and two teachers in Uvalde, Texas, in 2022, was a product of human imagination.

In *The Creative Spark: How Imagination Made Humans Exceptional*, anthropologist Agustín Fuentes shows how creativity and cooperation have worked hand in hand in the evolution of the human species: "No other animal exhibits the same intensity, constancy, and complexity that we see in our own cooperation." But Fuentes also cautions that these same propensities can "underlie the most horrific events."

What, then, would liberating imagination look like? Schools could grow our hearts, not just our minds, helping us reimagine who and what we value. Take Finland, a country that has bucked the prevailing norms and fashions in education by outlawing formal exams before the age of eighteen, refusing to segregate students by ability, and eliminating school selection, all of which reinforce social inequality.

Perhaps even more radical, students do not begin formal academics until the age of seven, and only then are they introduced to reading, writing, and math in school. Until then, the focus is on play, making friends, communicating, problem-solving, learning risk and responsibility, and the joy of learning, with a mix of free play and teacher-directed play carefully organized to support children's growth and well-being.

Once in secondary school, school hours are shorter, homework is light, and students receive a fifteen-minute outdoor break for every hour of class time. "Teaching to the test" is an alien concept. Yet, when it comes to educational assessments across economically developed countries, the Finns are at or near the top of international rankings. Go figure, *not* fixating on tests ends up yielding higher test scores.

But these outcomes are the result not only of Finnish emphasis on creativity and equity but also the country's investment in robust social security and public health programs, including free school meals for all students. Crucially, too, educators are trained well, paid well, and respected. As professor of education at the University of Helsinki Gunilla Holm says: "The goal is that we should all progress together."

WHEN IT COMES TO reimagining the relationship between the economy and society, Arturo Escobar, author of *Designs for the Pluriverse: Radical Interdependence, Autonomy, and the Making of Worlds*, points to the "forceful emergence of transition narratives, imaginaries, and proposals" among scholars and activists alike. Alternatively dubbed "transition discourses" and "transition designs," Escobar points to philosopher and priest Ivan Illich's 1973 invitation to move "from industrial to convivial societies." In the Global North, the aim is to transition from market-centric economies to ones characterized by *degrowth*. Not simply about doing "less of the same," degrowth is about "living with less *and* differently, about downscaling while fostering the flourishing of life in other terms."

Transition imaginaries, Escobar points out, are different depending on the history and circumstances of where you live. In the Global South, one of the ways they are framed is Buen Vivir—or "Good Living" and collective well-being (*sumak kawsay* in Quechua). Emerging from the struggles of Indigenous communities, people of African descent, peasants, and others, Buen Vivir "subordinates economic objectives to the criteria of human dignity, social justice, and ecology." Rather than conceive of degrowth and Buen Vivir as separate processes, one happening in the Global North and the other in the South, Escobar sees them as "fellow travelers" in a larger planetary transition.

Importantly, transition imaginaries are concerned not only with restructuring the world *out there* but with transforming the worlds *in here*—our identities, our psyches, our spirits. "The historical mission of our time," according to Thomas Berry, "is to reinvent the human—at the species level, with critical reflection, with the community of life systems . . . by means of story and shared dream experience." Instead of *Homo economicus*—or the "dollar hunting animal" who makes decisions based on cost-benefit analyses guided purely by self-interest (a fabled abstraction concocted by economists and kept alive by those who worship selfishness and justify human greed and guile)—we have *Homo cooperativus*, with study after study demonstrating how much humans care about fairness and reciprocity. "Survival of the friendliest," as one observer calls it, rescripting the story of human evolution, shining a light on how our development as a species has relied on prosocial actions and decisions for the collective good.

Moving forward, then, requires remembering who we are.

What's more, any "reinvention of the human" must wrestle with the fact that we have not *all* been welcomed into the category of human. Systems of extraction and "growth" in the forms of slavery, colonialism, and capitalism have distorted, degraded, and denied the humanity of so many people. The historical mission of our time must entail, then, an honest reckoning with the existing stratification of humanity as a starting point for any reinvention. We must rewrite the story in which, as Jamaican philosopher Sylvia Wynter has described, one genre of human, *The Man*, "white-heterosexual-breadwinner-and-measuring-stick-of-human-normalcy," has subordinated all others, leading to the social and ecological catastrophes we now face.

For some, talk of "reinventing the human," or resuscitating *Homo cooperativus*, may be too far out there, too *outlandish* even, in the face of so much human greed and brutality. For others of you, the challenges ahead feel too daunting. Yes, but so is lurching from one crisis to the next until, finally, there is no in-between, no time to catch our breath, no cease-fire, and calamity and turmoil are all there is, until earth itself becomes one giant hashtag: #TheEnd.

While we still seem to be caught in the treacherous segue between stories, those cast as victims in old master narratives are writing themselves anew. Remember the Doctrine of Discovery? On July 28, 2022, a large procession of Indigenous protesters made their way inside Canada's national shrine in Quebec City, where Pope Francis was scheduled to hold a mass as part of his nationwide tour. He was there to apologize for the role of the Catholic Church in the country's brutal Indian residential school system, in which an estimated 150,000 Indigenous children were stolen from their families, many of whom were physically and sexually abused, with at least 4,000 dying under horrendous conditions. Those gathered in silent protest held aloft a giant banner that read, in bold red and black letters, "Rescind the Doctrine," referring to the Doctrine of Discovery that was still in place.

In Latin, *rescindere* means "annul, cancel, abolish, remove by cutting off." *Rescind*, not simply *regret*. *Annul*, not simply *apologize*. *Abolish*, not simply *empathize*. Why? Because unless the old scripts animated by false notions of superiority and inferiority are ripped to shreds, we will be caught in an endless purgatory: forced to inhabit the same tired roles as we advance predictable and deadly plots. Instead, let us clear the way for new stories! Let us follow the example of the Indigenous protesters who demand that we smash death-making structures and construct new ones that give us life.

Imagination creates the situation,
and then, the situation creates the imagination.
It may, of course, be the other way around:
Columbus was discovered by what he found.

—James Baldwin

CHAPTER THREE

IMAGINING EUGENICS

———

"NOT EVERYONE CAN have a mansion. Not everyone can have a home theater. These are things we can simulate, to some degree, in virtual reality," says virtual reality (VR) developer John Carmack. "Most of the people in the world live in cramped quarters that are not what they would choose to be if they had unlimited resources." But how about a reality where everyone has *sufficient* resources? Instead of imagining a world where gross extremes between the wealthy and poor are ended, a growing industry fueled by the imagination of the uber-rich is working overtime to create virtual escapes from inequality and sell us on their dreams.

When questioned about plugging people into a fantasy world, Carmack responded, "I live in Dallas. It's 100 degrees there. We change the world around us in all that we do. We live in air-conditioning. People don't generally go, 'Oh, you're not experiencing the world around you because of air-conditioning.' . . . That is what human beings do, we bend the world to our will."

I read Carmack's statement in the middle of an unprecedented winter storm during which, at one point, four million Texans had no power. At least 246 people died, including eleven-year-old Cristian Pavon, whose mother found him frozen to death under the blankets in their unheated mobile home, his death later attributed to carbon monoxide poisoning precipitated by the storm and outage. And there was Jackie Pham Nguyen, who lost her mother and three children in a house fire as they tried to keep warm around the fireplace during the blackout—none of them were able to *bend the world to their will.*

The Texas blackouts, which hit Black and Latinx communities especially hard as utility companies prioritized keeping power on in richer areas, were a predictable byproduct of a deregulated electricity market that values profit over people. In the midst of this tragedy, many Texans received bills that were ten thousand times higher than normal, $450 a day in some cases. So, while the rich dream about virtual reality, this is the nightmare so many people are forced to endure in real life.

"We're way closer to *The Matrix* than people realize," says VR developer Gabe Newell. Human beings plugged in as batteries to power a virtual reality—this is what the techno-elite long for because it is *their* imagination into which we get plugged.

Meanwhile, back in Texas, many residents were dealing with the real reality: senior citizens who lacked basic internet access, where almost all emergency information was being transmitted, those without cars unable to reach "warming centers," people freezing in their beds, mothers weeping over the charred remains of their children. But, *yay*, we can put on VR headsets and forget all our worries. So, if the imaginations of tech oligarchs cannot save us, what is the alternative?

"The first step towards reimagining a world gone terribly wrong," implores Arundhati Roy, "would be to stop the annihilation of those who have a different imagination . . . outside of capitalism as well as communism. An imagination which has an altogether different understanding of what constitutes happiness and fulfillment."

Racism, among other axes of domination, helps produce this fragmented imagination—misery for some and monopoly for others. Those who want to construct a different social reality, one grounded in justice and joy for everyone, must first face social reality instead of escaping to a virtual reality designed by Silicon Valley. As André 3000 rapped, "I swear it don't cost much to pay attention to me / I tell like it is / then I tell it how it could be."

Although there are many different imaginaries vying for dominance, in this chapter we will home in on the ubiquity of a *eugenics imagination*, as it warps so many areas of our lives. Most people associate eugenics (from the Greek for "good in birth") with a fixed era, that of Nazi Germany, and with egregious medical practices, like forced sterilization. We do not usually think of our contemporary society as eugenic. But look closer . . . from who gets access to scarce resources when hospitals don't have enough supplies for all patients, to who gets warehoused in U.S. jails because they cannot afford bail, some lives are deemed desirable and others disposable. We can describe eugenics policies and practices in two ways. *Negative eugenics* seeks to limit the reproduction of those with undesirable traits, whereas *positive eugenics* encourages the propagation of those with desirable traits.

But it is too easy to only blame the eugenic systems *out there* without also examining how our private thoughts and judgments reflect and reproduce a dominant imagination that values specific lives over others. The first, perhaps most difficult, step toward exorcising eugenic ideas from our institutions is by reckoning with the ways that white supremacy, patriarchy, ableism, and class oppression have molded our innermost thoughts and desires. Our mental structures shape and are shaped by social structures, which means a change in one has the potential to impact the other.

TAKE OUR EDUCATIONAL SYSTEM, in which tracking, standardized testing, IQ tests, and gifted programs—as explored in this book's introduction—are employed to stratify young people, and which many of us still prop up as meaningful indicators of a student's value and potential. These practices persist despite open talk of their cultural and class bias, but with little acknowledgment of the eugenic roots of the field of statistics and IQ testing.

In his essay "How Eugenics Shaped Statistics," applied mathematical researcher Aubrey Clayton reveals how the ideas and methods of science pioneers Francis Galton and Karl Pearson (after whom are named some of the most common statistical terms) were animated by a deep-seated racist imagination that explicitly viewed white people as superior to all other groups.

Half-cousin of Charles Darwin, Galton was born into the British aristocracy and, as such, misapplied the principles of evolution to human traits like "lunacy, feeble-mindedness, habitual criminality, and pauperism." A proponent of both positive and negative eugenics, Galton thought the state should encourage white, rich elites to propagate while discouraging the reproduction of those he considered undesirables. To support his political agenda, he marshaled the "objectivity" of statistical analysis to create a "galaxy of genius." Credited with developing ideas fundamental to statistics, like regression and correlation, Galton was a major proponent of eugenicist breeding. He advocated, for example, a "Holy War against customs and prejudices that impair the physical and moral qualities of our race."

Turning to Karl Pearson, Clayton calls him the "eugenics movement's greatest holy warrior." A graduate of Cambridge University, Pearson became a professor of applied mathematics at University College London, where he encountered Galton and became his longtime collaborator. According to Pearson, "History shows me one way, and one way only, in which a high state of civilization has been produced, namely the struggle of race with race, and the survival of the physically and mentally fitter race." Pearson argued that it was "a false view of human solidarity, a weak humanitarianism, not a true humanism, which regrets that a capable and stalwart race of white men should replace a dark-skinned tribe which can neither utilize its land for the full benefit of mankind, nor contribute its quota to the common stock of human knowledge."

Today most people would not openly espouse eugenic thinking in such crude terms. Yet many of our policies and everyday social practices reflect a warrior's ambition to crush those deemed feeble and uplift those who are powerful and considered strong. Think of how many of our workplaces and schools rushed back to business as usual during the Covid-19 pandemic, risking the lives of those who were already immunocompromised and ignoring the hardships experienced by those newly affected by long Covid. Business as usual is often a way to impose a perverse political and moral calculus while depicting it as "common sense." As Clayton aptly observes, "The most consistent hallmark of someone with an agenda, it seems, is the excessive denial of having one."

Further, both old-school and contemporary eugenics are viewed through a distorted lens—framed and understood by proponents as part of a "progressive" movement. Pearson, for example, thought of it as "the directed and self-conscious evolution of the human race." That is, he assumed eugenics was a positive force in human and social development, helping the elite create a stronger society by weeding out the unfit and allowing the stronger to remain. I think this should lead us to question what popular ideas circulating today are actually eugenic wolves in "progressive" clothing.

In my tracing of the significance of scientists such as Galton and Pearson, you may be wondering, is it possible to separate the science from the scientist? Unlike toppling Confederate monuments, ridding statistics of the ghosts of its founders is not easy. "Statistical thinking and eugenicist thinking are, in fact, deeply intertwined," explains Clayton. For example, in one of his first calculations, Pearson set out to measure ancient skulls, concluding that the distribution in size implied the presence of two races that differed in intelligence and character. In a later study he turned to Jewish immigrant children, measuring their bodies, surveying their home environments, and administering intelligence tests. The conclusion? "The children (especially girls) were on average less intelligent than their non-Jewish counterparts, and their intelligence was not significantly correlated with any environmental factor that could be improved." Pearson's aim? To provide scientific justification for limiting immigration to only those of "superior stock."

Significance testing, often treated as the key scientific indicator for determining if a relationship between factors is "real" and not occurring by chance, was developed to advance eugenicist arguments about different racial groups. Today, there is a growing consensus among statisticians that the pursuit of "statistical significance" is not a scientific test but more of a philosophical one. Or perhaps we might call it an *imaginative* test, one with often severe consequences.

Policies excluding immigrants, promoting sterilization of non-whites, the poor, and people with disabilities, and preventing marriages across racial groups and within the same sex were all defended using the scholarly justifications of people like Galton, Pearson, and other scientific luminaries. In a continuous feedback loop, the eugenics imagination shaped science, and the sciences have been used to embolden eugenics policies. For students going into STEM fields, then, it is important to reckon with how this history impacts the present rather than pretend that so-called "hard" sciences are apolitical and innocent.

As recently as 2009, Jason Richwine, a PhD candidate in Harvard University's Department of Public Policy, wrote a dissertation, which was accepted, arguing that stricter U.S. immigration policies are justified on the grounds that Hispanics have lower IQs than whites. "The result," he explains, "is a lack of socioeconomic assimilation, and an increase in undesirable outcomes such as underclass behavior and loss of social trust. The upside is that calling attention to this problem may help focus policy on attracting a different kind of immigrant—the poor with great potential," or as he describes them in the dissertation abstract, "high-IQ immigrants."

Richwine advocates for IQ selection as the basis of

immigration, but he suggests calling it a "skill-based" policy to avoid negative reaction. This is exactly how the Heritage Foundation, his former employer, frames their proposal to decrease the numbers of low-skilled immigrants and increase those of high-skilled ones. We witness how, euphemized and weaponized, a racist eugenic imagination gets encoded in statistical methods and animates social policies.

Even when race-ethnicity is not explicitly mentioned, as it was by Richwine, sorting and ranking people in our "scored society" can still have deleterious consequences in people's lives. Sociologist Tamara K. Nopper compares the traditional credit-scoring companies with new marketplace lenders who construct what she terms "digital character." The latter is based on borrowers' online search engine history and social media activity, including how many friends they have and how often they interact with them, "as an indicator of stability." Proponents call it a more "holistic" means to assess creditworthiness, a way to include the "unbanked" and "underbanked," those with a thin credit file with little data, and an innovative method to financially include those who are left out of our scored society.

But while we might like to think of digital character as a color-blind alternative to old-school forms of sorting and ranking, Nopper urges us to question these newfangled forms of credit scoring built on nonfinancial consumer behavior on and off-line. The seeming neutrality, and liberal veneer, of new risk assessment tools brings us right back to the "progressive" commitments of those early eugenicists. A closer examination reveals how new credit-scoring models that produce digital character—what some pose as "alternative data," as it includes data beyond that factored into traditional credit-scoring models—could maintain the racial wealth gap and expose people to more pernicious forms of financial control.

Given that African Americans and Latinos are more likely to be unbanked, they would have to relinquish more privacy and expose themselves to more digital surveillance than their white and Asian American counterparts, to be financially included. For those who are labeled "high-risk" by these proprietary algorithms, they could become the target for subprime predatory loans. Worse still, this more "holistic" data collection and assessment makes it even harder for borrowers to refute faulty information and challenge discriminatory lending. Many have rightly argued that this scenario is worse than having no credit at all.

In a 2021 letter to the U.S. House of Representatives Committee on Financial Services, Nopper underscores this concern. In it, she says the problem is not only that digital character is more "subjective" than the supposedly "scientific" FICO score, nor even that it could exacerbate social disparities. Instead, she argues that a for-profit lending system is rotten at the root. Nopper invites us to expand our imagination to consider not only a public credit registry but the possibility of eliminating credit scoring altogether: "It would be bold, generative, and generous to consider what it would mean to design a socioeconomic system that does not require a 'scored society.'" Can you imagine an economy free of the eugenics imagination??

"I WAS LIKE, *OH my God, that's not right.* Do they think they're animals, and they don't want them to breed anymore?" asked Crystal Nguyen, who was formerly incarcerated at Valley State Prison in Chowchilla, California. Nguyen was one of many women who spoke with journalist Corey G. Johnson as part of his investigation into prison sterilization. Nguyen had been working in the infirmary at the time she observed a troubling pattern—doctors performing tubal ligations on incarcerated people, especially those who had served prison time before.

In 2013, Johnson reported on these forced sterilizations happening in two California state prisons, documenting nearly 150 tubal ligations between 2006 and 2010, despite a 1994 federal law banning the practice in prisons if it involves federal funds. Only one of those with whom Johnson spoke had not felt pressured into the surgery. The other women were pushed to do so, some in circumstances that made it impossible to prevent the sterilization. Kimberly Jeffrey told Johnson she "resisted the pressure to get a tubal ligation done—pressure that she says came while she was under sedation and strapped to an operating table." This phenomenon is part of a much broader continuum of eugenics characterized not only by coercion and sterilization but also by experimentation and commercial interests seeking to test non-therapeutic products: "prisoners were scientists' guinea pigs of choice during the twentieth century . . . routinely incorporated into dangerous medical experiments that were unthinkable for other populations."

Promoters of the sterilization of women in prisons, meanwhile, take no pains camouflaging their disdain for poor, nonwhite, and/or disabled people. Perhaps because disposable populations are already so weighted down with stigma and scorn, casting them outside the category of "human" seems to come with no serious consequence.

Eugenics can also be profitable for its proponents, as when the California Department of Corrections and Rehabilitation paid surgeons almost $150,000 over a ten-year period to sterilize incarcerated people from 1997 to 2010. Former OB-GYN for Valley State Prison James Heinrich justified his involvement, saying, "Over a 10-year period, that isn't a huge amount of money compared to what you save in welfare paying for these unwanted children—as they procreated more." This is the eugenic imagination unvarnished and unapologetic, shaping the profession of medicine and the carceral system.

Writing about a documentary, *Belly of the Beast*, that draws upon Johnson's investigation, one observer stated, "Instead of performing typical liberal disbelief around the discovery that eugenic sterilization persists today, *Belly of the Beast* shows how the very practice springs forth from the U.S. project and *white American imagination* [emphasis added]." But what do we know of the imaginations of those who are trapped, warehoused, and tortured in U.S. jails and prisons? This is something we will explore shortly through the work of scholar Nicole Fleetwood and her book, *Marking Time: Art in the Age of Mass Incarceration*. But first . . .

In the film *The Creative Brain*, neuroscientist David Eagleman describes creativity as a "superpower that we all possess," the "most potent, transformative tool that we have at our disposal," and not the "preserve of an elite few. Creativity is what humans do." And while the majority of those profiled in the documentary are superstar architects, inventors, musicians, and writers, there is a segment that celebrates the "healing power of creativity" by briefly profiling people locked up in Louisiana's Lafayette Correctional Facility.

An unnamed Black man who participates in the prison's creative writing program reflects, "I find myself when I write, I create a whole 'nother world. The one I'm supposed to be living in."

Eagleman declares, in turn, "This transformation has a real-world effect. Prisoners who take part in creativity-based programs are up to 80 percent less likely to reoffend." Incarcerated people, instead of being completely amputated from our collective imagination, get an opportunity to "redeem" themselves through their creative efforts.

Novelist and English professor Zachary Lazar, who teaches creative writing in Louisiana prisons, noticed that many of his students were artists, musicians, rappers, and tattoo artists. He speculates that many people may wind up in prison because it is hard to earn a living through creative pursuits. "There was a huge abundance of creative people in that prison," Lazar observed. "It just seemed so obvious to me that part of the way of preventing people from being in prison is to harness that creativity somehow."

This reminds me of the dystopian novel *Never Let Me Go* by Kazuo Ishiguro, in which sympathetic human clones attempt to establish their personhood through their artistic works. *Could a creature without a human spirit create such heart-wrenching paintings?* they seem to ask. Yet their appeals are ultimately rejected, exquisite art be damned. And the clones must ultimately undergo "completion," to be killed to supply organs to non-cloned humans. Dystopias, whether fictional or real, depend on euphemisms to filter reality.

Returning to *The Creative Brain*, despite the film's attempt to celebrate creativity in different forms, there is something uneasy about its depiction of those held captive. The focus seems to be less on their creative process or their works of art and more on how *they* are being re-created by engaging with this "groundbreaking" program. That is, the credit for innovation seems to go to those who offer prison arts programs, not the imprisoned artists.

But, we might ask, does the creative process transform the brutal institution of prison or does it hide that brutality? Alas, I think we should be wary of the proposition that arts are an antidote to the evils of incarceration. The celebration of such programs often promotes a narrative of individual rehabilitation and productivity, which in turn can gloss over a violent carceral apparatus that targets and ensnares poor and nonwhite people in a too-often deadly embrace.

The prison, after all, is a eugenic institution, snatching up and discarding those society deems *human detritus*. Children who grow up in the poorest U.S. zip codes have the highest rates of incarceration and, according to the Sentencing Project, Black youth are four times more likely to be locked up than their white peers. It is not only that formerly incarcerated people are shut out of the labor market but that jails and prisons warehouse the poor, rounding up those in "dispossessed districts" and criminalizing those confined to "castaway categories," like "homeless," "drug addict," "sex worker," and "unemployed." Indeed, economists Adam Looney and Nicholas Turner found that almost half of all incarcerated men were unemployed three years before their incarceration, and those who did work earned on average $6,250 a year.

In her book *Marking Time: Art in the Age of Mass Incarceration*, scholar and art curator Nicole Fleetwood explains how "prison thrives on limiting the field of vision of imprisoned people and the nonincarcerated public. . . . Each is positioned to see only a fragment of the labyrinthine system." It is not just the unabashed ambassadors of modern-day eugenics who contribute to this fragmentation. Fleetwood also calls attention to the "fraught imaginaries" of nonprofit prison art collaborations. The problem with nonprofits is that while many are well-intentioned, they are at the whim of what donors want and what prison administrators will agree to. Not to mention, most of these nonprofits rose to prominence through, and now often retain funding from, the increase in prison populations.

While the proliferation of nonprofit prison art collaborations may seem like a promising alternative to total creative deprivation in carceral facilities, scholar Baz Dreisinger describes the trend as "smoke screens, obstructing our view of the big picture, which is that when it comes to justice and safety and human treatment, prisons simply don't make sense." So, we must consider what it takes to clear our vision and behold a bigger picture that includes incarcerated and formerly incarcerated people as protagonists in their own stories and co-builders of our collective future.

Speaking at Art for a New Future, a symposium held in the summer of 2021, visual artist Ndume Olatushani recounted his frustrations in developing his craft while incarcerated. Olatushani, who was wrongfully convicted of first-degree murder and spent twenty-eight years in prison (twenty of those on death row), explained, "Locking people up in this country is a huge industry . . . so helping me be a better person, and be a productive person when I come home, that's against the bottom line. . . . It's all part of this strategy to disconnect the people that's behind these walls and fences from the people outside," hardening the distinction between law-abiding citizens and so-called criminals.

Art becomes disruptive behind bars, not simply by "proving" the humanity of those held captive (as in *Never Let Me Go*) but because it challenges the *inhumanity* of the system and creates a connection between those inside and outside prison walls. One of the main ways art can disrupt the carceral imagination is by refuting the eugenic classification and fragmentation of people—desirable or deplorable, worthy or disgraced, precious or superfluous. Art can remind us who we are beyond the trappings of privilege or prison.

One of Olatushani's paintings depicts a girl four or five years old, mahogany skin, hair braided, sweetly clad in a white top, salmon-pink shorts, and matching hat. Purple flowers and a single butterfly hover near her feet where she tiptoes, looking over a white picket fence. The girl, Olatushani explains, is looking across for the proverbial "greener grass." Like so many of us, she doesn't realize what she already has, a realization that helped Olatushani survive dehumanizing conditions by finding freedom within.

FROM PRISONS TO PLAYGROUNDS, we can bear witness to how Black childhood and thus Black imaginations are policed. But, as we develop keener vision, we can also observe how Black children continue to find ways to imagine, dream, and play by *all* means necessary. In her dissertation, based on three summers of ethnographic research in Atlanta, Georgia, from 2018 to 2020, educator and community organizer Ariana Brazier shows us both sides of this process—suppression *of* and innovation *by* impoverished Black youth.

These youth are born into environments of state-sanctioned deprivation, or "organized abandonment," as political geographer Ruth Wilson Gilmore calls it. Starting in infancy, impoverished children and communities experience what researchers term *play deprivation*—few opportunities to play, which negatively impacts their mental, emotional, and physical well-being. In under-resourced and understaffed daycare centers, Black and Brown children are often strapped into rockers and high chairs for prolonged sedentary periods, at an age when they need ample "tummy time." In childhood, they are corralled into schools where recess time is a tease, and art and physical education programs have been cut due to decreased public investment in education. With no way to release their energy or exercise their imaginations, students are disciplined with punitive zero-tolerance policies that prepare them for a lifetime sentence in a carceral society.

One of the seventh graders in Brazier's study, Julio, lamented: "School feel like prison—we here all the time." Another middle-school student corrected him: "No, it feels like juvie." Paradoxically, many of these disciplinary policies are akin to the progressive vision espoused by eugenicists like Karl Pearson, justifying harsh discipline as a means to "close academic disparities." Schooling becomes standardized testing without creative expression, arbitrary rules without room to breathe, Black Excellence without Black Joy.

Meanwhile, standing wait in their neighborhoods, police are primed and ready to disrupt Black leisure with stop-and-frisk, targeted harassment, and violence. And that's on a *good* day. For twelve-year-old Tamir Rice, shot dead on a Cleveland playground over a pellet gun that Officer Timothy Loehmann claimed was a threat, play was transformed into danger, and Tamir paid with his life.

More recently, in the Bronx on July 21, 2022, teenager Raymond Chaluisant was playing with a bead blaster—a toy air gun that shoots gel water beads—when off-duty correctional officer Dion Middleton shot Chaluisant in the face, killing him. Soon after, the NYPD launched a social media campaign criminalizing toy guns, instead of penalizing trigger-happy cops.

As Brazier documents, city housing authorities and real-estate developers collude to interrupt Black childhood by designing spaces and building barriers within and around neighborhoods that make it hard to play freely. "Black children's physical and creative movements threaten the hierarchical social order that requires passivity and resignation," she explains. Black children are *adultified* by the carceral state and *infantilized* by the welfare state. Everywhere they turn, they are denied the ability to just *be*.

Even if there are no fences towering overhead to barricade people in or no police hovering nearby to interrupt play, there are still few safe spaces in neighborhoods characterized by "advanced marginality," a term used by sociologist Loïc Wacquant. By this, he means the way impoverished Black communities are not only cut off from resources and institutions that are conducive to safety and well-being, but how residents of these communities are also *amputated from the collective imagination* of the nation.

Yet, as we will observe in the next chapter, many of these children still *make a way outta no way*. More on that shortly. But now. . . .

It is not only Black childhood that is the target of the eugenic imagination but an illusory "innocent childhood," which is conjured and weaponized in the exercise of racist policies and practices. In *Racial Innocence: Performing American Childhood from Slavery to Civil Rights*, historian Robin Bernstein begins with the case of Keith Bardwell, a Louisiana justice of the peace who refused, in 2009, to marry a white woman, Beth Humphrey, and a Black man, Terence McKay, and justified his anti-miscegenation stance by saying, "I do it to protect the children. The kids are innocent and I worry about their futures."

But, as Bernstein points out, the children Bardwell invokes are

figments of his imagination; these "imagined children deserve protection more than living adults deserve constitutional rights," she
writes. We are forced to accept, then, that our imaginations are not
simply a force for good in the world, a capacity that we develop and
then set free. Rather, given the power to do harm through oppressive
imaginaries of all types, we must critically examine, challenge, and
potentially purge our imaginations whenever they become infected
by a "fatal coupling of power and difference."

Imagination, we might say, is the invisible circuitry that connects
the world *out there* to our inner worlds. So, we cannot just be critical
of oppressive systems without also examining how our own private
thoughts and desires reflect and reproduce a dominant imagination
that values some lives over others. We must, in a sense, continuously
deprogram ourselves, challenging the hierarchies that place us above
or below, and decode the imaginative justifications that make those
social hierarchies seem natural, durable, and deserved.

ACCORDING TO A Deloitte Digital Media Trends survey, of all
the different types of entertainment enjoyed by young people ages
fourteen to twenty-four (so-called Gen Z), video games are the
most popular activity (26 percent), followed by listening to music
(14 percent), browsing the internet (12 percent), and engaging
with social media (11 percent). A majority said video games helped
them stay connected to peers during the Covid-19 lockdowns. Yet,
like other forms of media, greater connection also means greater
exposure to the "racism, misogyny, and xenophobia within game
culture." As communications scholar Ergin Bulut puts it, "Game
workers have a problem."

In "White Masculinity, Creative Desires, and Production

Ideology in Video Game Development," Bulut explains that games and other tech products are often coded as "supposedly neutral technological system[s]." In reality, "white masculinity informs game workers' professional discourses, technological practices, ludic desires, and imaginations . . . white masculine fantasies condition game developers' creative desires to unleash escapism on computer screens." But what does that imagination entail?

According to Bulut, who conducted three years of ethnographic fieldwork at a U.S.-based studio he calls Desire, the main product is a game allowing players to "entertain themselves in urban America with exotic experiences" of gritty violence and mayhem. Most of the time Desire programmers described the appeal of the game in terms of "escapism," "letting out your inner child," and the "general freedom to do what you want." A few acknowledged that it enabled people who grew up in suburbia, themselves included, to engage in "identity tourism."

A programmer of color, Matthew, admitted, "We're definitely playing off of stereotypes of [Black urban] culture regardless of whether those stereotypes are actually true or not. It's a romanticized vision of what that culture is. And the truth is that culture includes a lot of nasty stuff."

In defending the game's offensive narrative, Stuart (white, early thirties) responded, "We offend everybody. We go after men. We go after women. We go after fat. We go after skinny. We go after white, black, Asian, Latino. It doesn't matter to us. I think that's what allows us to get away with it. It's the fact that we go after everybody equally."

Here we see how a white masculine imagination *flattens* social reality. *Equal Opportunity Offense* is the prime directive, and durable hierarchies are figments of others' imagination. By imagining the world in this way, the designers refuse to acknowledge that the epithets, stereotypes, and abuse of some groups inside virtual worlds are buttressed, underwritten, and cosigned by policies and practices outside the game. Most importantly, the white masculine subjectivity is one that *erases its own existence*: "Going after everyone equally erases white masculinity's political responsibility precisely because whiteness powerfully remains unnoticed as a world of habit," writes Bulut.

To be sure, the escapism-cum-domination of white men's imagination is not simply a product of gaming culture. It is much older and vaster. A eugenic way of imagining the world, wherein some places and people are deemed inherently inferior and thus requiring domination, has justified colonialist expansion, slavery, and genocide. It gives new meaning to scholars Wendy Chun and Andrew Lison's notion that "fun is a battlefield," when actual battlefields were some of the first sites of gaming.

The entertainment value of eugenics, in turn, is not paradoxical but contributes to its durability, expansiveness, and creators' plausible deniability. Desire and disdain often go hand in hand. Drawing upon the work of philosophers Gilles Deleuze and Felix Guattari, Bulut writes, "Desire is the libidinal infrastructure that fuels capitalist social relations. There is nothing unreal or irrational about desire." Lust and longing are encoded into the zeros and ones of video games, animating the algorithmic architecture that enables identity tourism and escapism in digital worlds.

But is that the only way to imagine gaming? Anthropologist Akil Fletcher says no. He points to Black Girl Gamers (BGG), created in 2015 by Jay-Ann Lopez, which has successfully carved out a protected digital space for over eight thousand members and eighty thousand followers amid the hostility endemic to white masculine gaming culture. BGG started out as a safe space where members could connect, play, and share technical skills on how to improve in video games. Now it is an international network that operates across multiple platforms, offering workshops, summits, and consulting services throughout the industry while continuing to employ rigorous methods of content moderation to prevent harassment online.

Computer and cognitive scientist D. Fox Harrell also takes a proactive approach to transforming digital media from within. In *Phantasmal Media: An Approach to Imagination, Computation, and Expression*, he analyzes the oppressive illusions, or *phantasms*, that infect our everyday experiences; he also designs computer systems that engender empowering images and ideas that allow for greater expression and self-fashioning in digital environments. He and his team have created a range of computer applications (Chameleonia: ShadowPlay, DefineMe: Chimera, and IdentityShare) that allow users to critically assess stigmatizing digital representations and to create avatars and online identities that are meaningful and authentic to themselves. Harrell cautions that when computer scientists rely on their own limited intuitions to design systems, rather than engage theories that show how identities are "enacted, contextual, imaginative, and infrastructural," they are likely to perpetuate patterns of discrimination and disenfranchisement. "We can do better," Harrell urges.

At the heart of our prevailing eugenics imagination is a deeply individualistic and hypercompetitive desire that, nonetheless, is born out of our longing for social acceptance. The irony, of course, is that acceptance is predicated on superiority—*I am more beautiful, more intelligent, wealthier, and healthier than the rest, and thus worthy of your love and admiration*. The question we face now is whether we can imagine a world in which social acceptance does not rest on these kinds of judgments. You belong without having to show proof of your fitness or superiority.

This solidaristic imagination is born not of individualism, but of interdependence, what disability studies scholar Rosemarie Garland-Thomson calls *inclusive world-building*. "I am because we are, we are because I am," goes the South African philosophy of ubuntu. This is more than "accommodating" people's differences on the edges. It requires recognizing that the world is round, that we *all* belong, and that we must structure society to reflect that underlying truth. Pie in the sky, you say? Too far-fetched and utopian? Well, for those currently living at the crossroads of multiple dystopias, "living in the real world" is what is truly impossible.

YEARS AGO, WHEN I first started to make sense of how design decisions shape social inequity, I used the metaphor of the park bench to make my point. Benches with armrests that kept people from lying down in Berkeley, California; single-occupancy benches that made people sit up in Helsinki, Finland; caged benches that deterred easy access in Angoulême, France; and my all-time favorite, the *spiked bench*—designed by German artist Fabian Brunsing—which required payment before the spikes would retract into the bench's surface. The latter's design invites us to think critically about the metering of social life, where only those who can pay are allowed to rest (or play). The spiked bench also highlights the eugenic imagination and all the ways it is embedded into the design of policies, platforms, and public infrastructure.

My preoccupation with benches as a parable for social life borders on obsession. Recently, I clicked on an image from a project by artist Sarah Ross. *Archisuits* consists of light-blue leisure jogging suits with foam appendages that allow individuals to fit into and onto structures that would otherwise be uncomfortable or impossible to use with ease.

While the spiked bench casts a critical light onto hostile structures, *Archisuits* takes the critique one step further, drawing attention to the ways individuals are expected to *accommodate* that hostility, through our dress, speech, and behavior, creating "work-arounds" that might make life a bit easier for the individual wearing the suit but do nothing to challenge the harmful status quo. The bench is a great metaphor for the spikes built into our institutions, while the foam-lined suit epitomizes how individuals are made responsible for being smarter, fitter, more *suitable*, to avoid harm. What, dear reader, are the foam suits you must wear to navigate hostile environments?

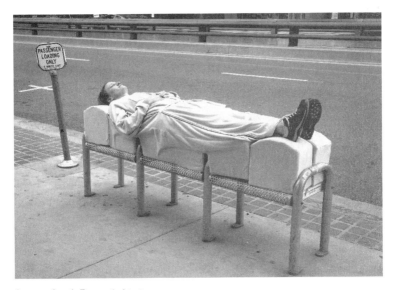

Source: Sarah Ross, *Archisuits*.

Here's one extreme example: a Back to School sale of bullet-proof book bags. Only $179.99, "the pack discreetly enhances your child's safety at school and on-the-go." They come in gray, aqua, and rose, and are made of DuPont's newest Kevlar technologies. "Ideal for elementary-aged students."

Can you imagine? I think about the children bleeding out under desks at Robb Elementary School, in Uvalde, Texas, in May 2022, the twenty-seventh school shooting of that year. I think about the Guard Dog Security Company and the uptick in sales of its bullet-proof book bags after the massacre. I wonder whether the Facebook algorithm directs ads for bulletproof bags only to customers in the Land of the Free. I think about the parents who don't have dispos-able income, those already hard-pressed to purchase basic school supplies like pencils and crayons, standing in the aisle looking at the $179.99 price tag (more than their combined monthly utility bills) for a lilac-colored bulletproof bag with a ~~lifetime~~ one year war-ranty. . . . more than their monthly utility bills. And I call *bullshit* on this "solution" to school shootings that have now become routine.

Is the Bullet Blocker NIJ IIIA Sprout Backpack a "failure of imagination," or simply the natural extension of a eugenic imagina-tion that displaces deadly social problems onto individuals, asking the most vulnerable to literally *shoulder* the problem?

Modern-day eugenics, after all, is "modern" precisely because it is often more subtle than the crude ranking and measuring of the skulls and noses of a previous generation, with its Better Babies and Fitter Family contests at county fairs. Nowadays, we allow hostile conditions to persist, and offer a plethora of products—from bul-letproof bags to healthcare—that promise to increase the chances of survival for those who can afford them. Rather than passing responsible gun laws, or investing in a stronger social safety net, or deepening connections in our communities, the suitable solution is wrapping our kids in Kevlar, arming our teachers with guns, and praying for the best.

In this way, modern-day eugenics enrolls each of us in its blood-soaked imagination—asking us to shoulder social problems, inviting us to purchase an illusion of safety, making any demand for robust public investment in the goods, services, and infrastructure required for everyone to live well appear unimaginable. The good news is that the eugenic imagination is not the only one. We can take off the hot, foam-padded suits we might wear in hopes of safety and belonging. We can transform the hostile environments that try to trap us—whether they are literal cages, barbed wire–encircled playgrounds, or bullet-friendly classrooms.

We can imagine otherwise.

The creative imagination has been colonized.

—Toni Cade Bambara

Think of yourself, Black creator,

freed of european restraint which first means

the restraint of self determined mind development. . . .

To imagine–to think–to construct–to energize!!!

—Amiri Baraka

CHAPTER FOUR

IMAGINING JUSTICE

———

W HEN I FIRST downloaded the app, I was wary. As someone who regularly climbs atop the "tech won't save us" soapbox, the idea that an augmented reality tool designed to celebrate the life of a young woman brutally slain by Louisville, Kentucky, police, tingled my antennae and put my skepticism on full alert. But since I personally knew and respected the app developer, Oakland-based curator Lady PheOnix, also known as Lady Phe, I gave it a try.

Sitting in my living room, raising the phone to eye level, a larger-than-life hologram of Breonna Taylor appeared in front of me. She was wearing a long, flowing iridescent gown, holding a bouquet of her favorite tulips, and all around her, flowers slowly bloomed and butterflies fluttered. When I walked closer, each flower held an audio message, starting with one by her younger sister, Ju'Niyah, until finally I had the opportunity to leave a message that future app users could hear. My living room had been transformed into a space to celebrate "Breonna's purpose, not her pain," as I would soon hear Lady Phe describe it.

On March 16, 2022, I joined Lady PheOnix, Ju'Niyah Taylor,

Kenneth Walker (Breonna's boyfriend who was there the night of the brutal assault), and the rest of the design team in Austin, Texas, for a panel at SXSW (South by Southwest), the premier festival celebrating art, tech, music, film, and education. In our discussion I would learn that, from a purely technical standpoint, the team had pushed the limits of AR and VR in developing an immersive augmented-reality experience. At the conference exhibit, individuals wearing a VR headset could walk around Breonna's bedroom, view her treasured belongings, and observe the artwork sent to her family from people around the world, which her family had curated for display in Breonna's real and virtual spaces. After the exhibit, conference-goers were able to attend our panel and hear from some of Breonna's loved ones, which moved some in the audience to tears.

After Breonna's killing, her family and friends were forced to grieve amid a never-ending stream of slanderous news reports and hateful online messages. This inspired Lady Phe to imagine a safe digital space to process sorrow and heartache: "She loved flowers. She loved adventure. She loved bringing people together and community and no one would know that by simply watching the news."

Ju'Niyah and Kenny, for their part, appeared genuinely invested in the project. It was a way to rewrite Breonna's story, scratching the contemptuous media speculation that she was responsible for her own death, and scripting a digital coda that extended her passion for nursing to one for collective healing. Breonna's Garden was designed to be a digital public space for celebrating life and gently holding grief; the app also provides a way for people to connect with others in honoring their deceased loved ones because the messages in the Garden can be for anyone, not just Breonna.

Even more than the technical innovations, what impressed me

was the care and collaboration that went into the design of Breonna's Garden. Lady Phe intentionally centered Breonna's family, including her mother, Tamika Palmer, and Ju'Niyah and Kenny, throughout the entire process. The Garden is, first and foremost, a place for her loved ones to find solace and a sanctuary.

Breonna's family continues to seek justice through the courts, and they began using the Garden to raise awareness that "Breonna still has not got justice," as Ju'Niyah put it, since the officers who shot her sister dead have not even been charged with a crime. On August 4, 2022, more than two years after Breonna was killed, four Louisville officers—three of whom provided false information that led to the nighttime raid and one of whom "fired blindly into Ms. Taylor's apartment from outside"—were charged by federal officials. The two officers who shot Breonna have still not been and are unlikely to be charged.

Lady Phe, in turn, encourages those of us who experience Breonna's Garden to expand our imaginations of justice to include the work of repair and healing. She draws upon the insights of educator Mia Mingus, who describes *transformative justice* as "a way of 'making things right,' getting in 'right relation,' or creating justice together." This view of justice does not only happen in the courts (if it happens there at all) but in community with others, even in digital communities, like Breonna's Garden, where people can gather and grieve, heal *and* organize.

It should be clear by now that our collective imagination has been arrested and confined, making it difficult to think beyond the racist, classist, sexist, ableist status quo. If ideologies are imagination + power, then the most effective ideologies are those that need no police to enforce them, because we internalize and perpetuate them ourselves. As Menominee educator and author Kelly Hayes tweeted, "A lot of things people say 'cannot be done' have not been meaningfully attempted in our context or our lifetimes. It's easy to maintain myths of impossibility when you crush all experiments."

In this chapter, we will shine a light on those who may at times feel crushed, but who crawl out from under the social structures bearing down on us, find others who want to do more than survive, and whisper to one another—"They tried to bury us, they didn't know we were seeds." Those who refuse to accept oppressive ideologies show us what is possible when we unleash our imaginations. We can rob unjust systems of their power and *make a way outta no way*—imagining different possibilities for how to connect and care for one another as we also remake the world.

PLAY CAN BE A matter of life and social death. In *Woke Gaming: Challenges to Oppression and Social Injustice*, editors Kishonna L. Gray and David J. Leonard admit that video games do not offer a "post-racism and post-misogyny promised land." Yet, while they are often tools of inequity, they can also be instruments of justice.

Take the game *Hair Nah* (as in "No, don't touch my hair"), developed by Momo Pixel, a Black woman. Players can customize avatars with different skin tones and hair styles—locs, braids, twists, perms. The goal is to fill the Nah! Meter by smacking away as many white hands, which are trying to touch the avatar's hair, as possible within 60 seconds. If you succeed, you level up to the next stage. The simplicity of the rules and resonant social commentary ensured that the game quickly went viral. Posts by Black women flooded Black Twitter; articles appeared in *Essence*, *Glamour*, and *Teen Vogue*, including coverage in Germany and South Africa, and messages poured into Momo's inbox, expressing gratitude for drawing attention to the daily forms of objectification that users experience. But there was also some backlash from the "All hair matters" crowd. Still, *Hair Nah* reminds us that liberatory countercurrents persist and that there are other ways to imagine ourselves and our relationship to each other if we look for them.

Remember Ariana Brazier's ethnography? In her fieldwork, Brazier noticed that children in Thomasville Heights Elementary School began "folding pieces of lined loose-leaf paper into dollar bill size folds, stacking them on top of each other, placing rubber bands around the stacks, then walking around school bragging about their 'fat stacks' (or their cash money)." In this make-believe world, the students "pretended they had large wads of cash that they continued to accumulate and eventually 'spend' as they traded larger stacks for cuts in line," among other things.

Brazier noted how many of the adults in the building deemed this creative play "wasteful" and "ghetto." But, for her, these "ghetto games" revealed something about young people's lived experiences, in which money was in short supply and where even the adults in their lives had very little economic power. In the real world, where no one around them had ready access to cash, these kids took it upon themselves to create their *own* cash system. *Genius.*

I think most of us intuit, at some level, that play can be therapeutic, helping us release stress and trauma. But I did not realize until encountering Brazier's work that play is a human right articulated in Article 31 of the 1989 UN Convention on the Rights of the Child, which the United States has yet to ratify. Remember Finland? There, play is integral to learning and socialization, rather than viewed as a luxury or indulgence. "The theorizing and processing that happens in play," Brazier writes, helps children develop "the skills and *imaginative force* necessary to confront oppressive ideologies that restrict their holistic development."

Despite the numerous forces colluding to deprive children of the right to play—from cutting recess and extracurriculars at school to unsafe neighborhoods and lack of green space—they continue to imagine and innovate abundance, prefiguring a world they want and need. Play allows them to "create new possibilities out of impossibilities."

Brazier's research shows how Black children, in particular, "play interactively, tell stories expressively, dance competitively, and laugh ostentatiously *even while* they grapple with societal imposition of oppressive ideologies." Those in authority imagine Black children as older, tougher, idler, more dangerous, more unruly, more culpable, more riotous, less worthy, and less sympathetic than they are. But, as in *Hair Nah*, we must slap away these brutish stories clawing at Black children's spirits. Our protection and cultivation of their imagination can be the difference between their self-actualization and their cultural annihilation.

IF THE REIGNING EUGENIC imagination in the United States depicts people in prisons as boogeymen, brutes, and monsters, those lurking in the shadows of our worst nightmares, then it is imperative that we imagine differently. Those who have been (or whose loved ones have been) warehoused under dreadful conditions recognize that the real monster is the carceral system itself, its many tentacles slithering into our neighborhoods, sirens blaring, knocking down our front doors, and dragging people out of their homes, dead or alive. "Assaultive and dehumanizing images" is how scholar Nicole

Fleetwood describes the dominant representation of those who are imprisoned. This "spectacular visual assault" helps justify mass incarceration and generate support for "tough crime policies and punitive sentencing."

Fleetwood wanted to turn those representations inside out by curating images crafted by and in collaboration with incarcerated individuals. In her book *Marking Time*, Fleetwood expands our field of vision and thus our collective imagination by engaging the art practices of those who are imprisoned. She asks, "Instead of distracting from or obfuscating the fundamental wrongness of prisons and caging, how can prison arts collaborations build *new imaginary horizons* by forming relations, ways of looking, and practices of interdependence that challenge the institutional brutality and punitive discourse separating the incarcerated from the nonincarcerated?"

When I joined Fleetwood for a virtual conversation about *Marking Time*, she spotlighted a number of the artists featured in the book, three of whom I introduce here: Mark Loughney made the cover image with selections from his series of over five hundred black-and-white graphite portraits, titled *Pyrrhic Defeat: A Visual Study of Mass Incarceration*. For the series, Loughney, who was imprisoned in the state of Pennsylvania for ten years, asked other incarcerated people to sit for twenty minutes while he sketched their faces.

The aesthetic refusal of solitary images, a literal *drawing together* of people experiencing the horrors of life under captivity, directly challenges the use of solitary confinement as a routine method of torture within prisons. It also challenges prison itself, as an anti-social institution, that isolates a "criminal race" (which includes *all* those held captive) from the broader society. Fleetwood has been intimately affected by this brutal function of the carceral state, as many of her relatives in southwest Ohio have been swept into the bowels of the beast, cutting her and her family members off from their loved ones trapped inside.

Another image that Fleetwood flashed on the screen during our conversation was Tameca Cole's collage and graphite portrait *Locked in a Dark Calm*. In it, two eyes, a nose, and a mouth peer out from behind a gray masklike collage, with the faint shadow of a body visible. Cole was abused by prison staff when she was incarcerated in Alabama. Anything she did to challenge that abuse was met with more abuse. As Fleetwood explained, Cole created "a space of calm, a space of her own vision of freedom, while also protecting herself psychically from the harm she was experiencing."

This image brings to mind the scene in the film *12 Years a Slave*, based on Solomon Northup's 1853 memoir. Patsey, played by Lupita Nyong'o, is sitting on the grass at the plantation, having experienced incredible violence and sexual abuse at the hands of her master. The camera zooms in to see her playing with a set of handmade dolls, crafted from what appears to be straw. In his memoir, Northup writes, "Patsey's life, especially after her whipping, was one long dream of liberty. Far away . . . she knew there was a land of freedom. . . . In her imagination it was an enchanted region, the Paradise of the earth." How else could she survive, could any of us survive, without the ability to envision a world, even if only with the companions we are able to conjure out of the earth, where we are free simply to be?

Finally, Fleetwood highlighted a work titled simply *Self-Portrait, 2016*. Artist Russell Craig created a ten-by-eight-foot image against the backdrop of a collage made from all of his criminal records, starting with his foster records at age five to documents from his release when he was in his early to mid thirties. Craig not only resists a "carceral biography" that seeks to reduce him to only those categories legible to the carceral state but he has reappropriated the reductive texts and violent imagery to reimagine himself whole, with a fresh haircut, edges, mustache, and goatee looking tight. Against the black-and-white text, which is reduced and illegible, his skin glows brown, as if the sun is shining directly on him, and his eyes are focused intently on the viewer, as if to ask, *Now can you see me?*

WHILE FLEETWOOD'S WORK WRESTLES with the power and potential of imagining justice together, other collaborations flatten and sanitize social reality.

In 2015, a partnership between Sidewalk Labs, an urban innovation company which at the time was under parent company Alphabet, and Waterfront Toronto, a revitalization nonprofit, announced redevelopment plans for Quayside, a 12-acre parcel of land on Toronto's eastern waterfront. Advanced as a "new model of inclusive urban development . . . striving for the highest levels of sustainability, economic opportunity, housing affordability, and new mobility," it was an experiment.

Sidewalk Labs planned to use the latest in "smart" technologies, including a vast network of sensors installed on the streets, buildings, public transit, parks, and even in people's homes "to help guide resource-efficient housing and traffic decision-making . . . a neighborhood built from the internet up," transforming the waterfront into what one reporter called a "high-tech utopia." But, as Toni Morrison once commented in a 1998 interview, "All paradises, all utopias are designed by who is not there, by the people who are not allowed in."

Sidewalk Labs was prepared to invest over $1 billion with plans to attract $38 billion more in private investment over two decades. For the public display of its plans, it used colorful slides that painted an "alluring urban scene" belying the " 'Big Brother'-esque . . . data-gathering infrastructure more or less built into the walls." The presentation showed "organic-looking outdoor spaces with lush palm fronds and multi-story outdoor terraces . . . multi-story structures." It was to be a net-zero energy development that emphasized walking, cycling, and slow-moving, environmentally friendly transit. In short, Sidewalk Labs crafted a captivating story.

Although Google proudly announced again and again how important public input was to the process, including soliciting feedback from 21,000 Torontonians, the project was hampered by widespread public opposition to its data harvesting and surveillance, even when done in the name of environmental sustainability, public health, and public safety. Many city residents disliked the proposed level of surveillance, however hidden and "greenwashed" by the smart city designs. More broadly, they expressed concerns about the privatization of public life. "A city is not a business," said civic tech advocate and outspoken critic of Sidewalk Labs Bianca Wylie.

After two years, the project came to a screeching halt. Sidewalk Labs' CEO, Daniel Doctoroff, gave the reason as Covid-19's unpredictable impact on the economy. But critics and agitators say the pandemic simply put the final nail in the coffin of an experiment that was faulty from the start. They point out that the project, from its inception, bypassed democratic processes and did not meaningfully address public concerns over a lack of affordable housing, the pervasive digital dragnet built into "every nook and cranny" of the proposed infrastructure or the company's own failure to grapple with existing forms of exclusion and inequity.

In an open letter to the board of directors of Waterfront Toronto, the nonprofit in charge of developing the land, Indigenous elders Duke Redbird and Calvin Brook said the company's actions reinforced "a pattern of tokenism and insincere engagement of Indigenous peoples in the planning process." None of their fourteen recommendations, like supporting the creation of an Indigenous school and Indigenous education programs, were adopted in the 1,500-page master plan, although lip service was paid in it to having had Indigenous input. Redbird stated, "It was just shocking that there was kind of a blatant disregard for all of the work that we did. They just wanted to check off a box that says, 'We did Indigenous consultation.'"

The city eventually withdrew from the redevelopment partnership, Toronto residents ultimately rejecting the neat, tidy, and aesthetically pleasing visions of techno-utopianists, whose computational dreams reduce the complexity of social life in urban environments, transforming political questions into technical challenges.

But that wasn't the end of Sidewalk Labs. The company's products are still used in piecemeal fashion in other cities. As Wylie cautions, it is not just products they are selling: "They are getting governments to procure entire business models, and thus act as both regulator and regulated. To state the obvious, it is undemocratic to have vendors set public policy."

For example, a Sidewalk Labs spinoff called Replica is using data and machine learning to inform city planning decisions across the country, piloted in Kansas City, Missouri, sold to the state of Illinois, and procured by Portland, Oregon, among others. But despite its promise to help develop more accessible transportation and services, city officials in Portland have been frustrated by Replica's lack of transparency when it comes to their documentation of data sources, methodology, and privacy safeguards. In other words, they want the data without the data governance.

If it had been successful, Sidewalk Labs would have brought to life a dream of ex–Alphabet CEO Larry Page, who, two years prior, had mused, "There are many exciting things you could do that are illegal or not allowed by regulation. And that's good, we don't want to change the world. But maybe we can set aside a *part* of the world."

In response to Page's statement, journalist Mat Honan wrote a speculative essay for *Wired*—"Welcome to Google Island"— about a lawless land of unbridled data collection through electrolyte water filled with microsensors, holographic Google Beings stitched together from people's online images, swarms of robotic spiders, and experiments with teleportation. As the (fictional) Page gives Honan a tour of Google Island, Page's Being muses about how democracy is so passé: "If democracy worked so well, if a majority public opinion made something right, we would still have Jim Crow laws and Google Reader." Instead of annoying distractions like the rule of law, Google Island is governed by information. "We believe we can fix the world's problems with better math. . . . All we need is an invitation."

As cognitive scientist Abeba Birhane warns, the entire computational enterprise is built on "solving problems." So, despite the messiness of social life, it can't help but approach everything in terms of "problem → solution," and whatever it cannot neatly contain gets left out or "stripped of their rich complexities."

But elsewhere, cities are being imagined with an eye toward complexity and social transformation.

In Spring 2021, I participated in a virtual conference hosted by

Stanford University's Center for Comparative Studies in Race and Ethnicity. A panel titled "A People-Centric Smart City for Racial Justice" included Francesca Bria, former chief technology officer for the city of Barcelona, where, in 2015, activist Ada Colau became mayor on a Green Deal platform "with a social justice vision at the very core of it."

As Bria put it, a people-first approach involves large-scale citizen participation and the democratic control of digital technology and data, rather than technological solutions. Big tech has unprecedented market power, more than the entire European stock market, but it also has unprecedented social power, both of which increased during the Covid-19 pandemic. A people-centered approach entails "turning data into a common good and into a public infrastructure. . . . It doesn't start with connectivity, data, sensors, artificial intelligence, algorithms. No, it starts with people." But what does that look like in practice?

For starters, it looks like over forty thousand Barcelona residents submitting proposals on everything from affordable housing to air quality to shape the government agenda, then many more participating in citizen assemblies and consultations to consider and implement those proposals.

It involves "integrating the collective intelligence of citizens in decision-making processes" through the use of digital participation platforms, like Decidim, alongside in-person neighborhood-level deliberation. Decidim Barcelona, which has been adopted by over eighty cities across twenty countries around the world, is an open-source, privacy-enhancing software "built with fundamental rights at its very core."

In Barcelona, a people-centric smart-city approach thus entailed ending contracts with companies that were harvesting citizens' data, and implementing a "data sovereignty" clause in all procurement contracts, which mandates that any providers with city contracts must transfer data in machine-readable format. They are also developing the means for citizens to control what data they share and what they want to keep private. "This is a new social pact—a new deal on data," says Bria.

Instead of "only two possible futures for the digital society," Big Tech and Big State, Barcelona is experimenting with a decentralized, democratic future in which citizens can decide the *if*, *when*, and *how* of data. It is part of a global movement, Cities Coalition for Digital Rights. Like schools, we can imagine cities as laboratories for incubating civic participation, digital stewardship, and sustainable alternatives where people have a genuine say in what futures take shape.

As tech columnist John Thornhill observed, the divergent trajectories of Toronto and Barcelona help us to imagine the relationship between technology and society anew: "This is a tale of two cities . . . that may hold important lessons for others around the world. Both have big ambitions to change the way they operate but reflect very different visions of how smart cities should be run."

Imagining justice closer to home, I look to the work of the People's Advocacy Institute (PAI) in Jackson, Mississippi. PAI spearheads a range of initiatives including participatory budgeting, violence interruption programs, community reinvestment, police accountability, and the Credible Messenger Program, which mobilizes community mentors who are "closest to the pain" and therefore "closest to the solution" to train and resource currently and formerly incarcerated young people. At the heart of all their work, PAI is committed to community-led governance and partners with the Jackson People's Assembly, a forum for residents to share ideas, connect with neighbors, and make plans to "make Jackson a city that works for all of us."

Since the Jackson water crisis, in 2022, when collapsing water-treatment infrastructure cut off safe drinking water to 150,000 residents, assembly deliberations have increasingly centered on how to offer short-term relief to residents while laying the groundwork for long-term infrastructure investment. "Let's Dream Together" is the welcome message that greets visitors to the People's Assembly homepage. This focusing on what *could* be amid the harsh realities of what *is* echoes Robin D. G. Kelley's entreaty: "We must tap the well of our own collective imaginations, that we do what earlier generations have done: dream. . . . Without new visions we don't know what to build, only what to knock down. We not only end up confused, rudderless, and cynical, but we forget that making a revolution is not a series of clever maneuvers and tactics but a process that can and must transform us."

Similarly, Leaders of a Beautiful Struggle (LBS) is a grassroots think tank based in Baltimore, Maryland, that is not interested in incremental reform or softening the jagged edges of violent systems but rather on creating transformative public policy by empowering residents to dream big. For example, LBS challenges the "non-profit industrial complex," which they charge with profiting off Black suffering. By establishing the Baltimore Children and Youth Fund, LBS offers an alternative community-centered grant process that can be adapted to other locales. The fund invests in youth leadership development, violence prevention, technical assistance programs, and more.

The People's Advocacy Institute and Leaders of a Beautiful

Struggle are two among many organizations imagining and materializing justice by combining the fight for social, political, and economic self-determination with the vital work of freedom dreaming. This is part of a radical tradition of people who have no interest in being "included" inside a burning house. Instead, they are sounding the alarm about the treacherous blaze while, at the same time, laying down the bricks for more habitable social structures. We can each join in this work of world-building, if we choose.

Pragmatism and imagination, policy change and speculative vision need not be at odds. In *Octavia's Brood: Science Fiction Stories from Social Justice Movements*, coeditor Walidah Imarisha writes, "Whenever we try to envision a world without war, without violence, without prisons, without capitalism, we are engaging in speculative fiction. All organizing is science fiction." Indeed, there are countless movements around the world, from Cairo to Ferguson, that have been inspired by movements for freedom and self-determination à la the Black Panthers and that deploy "next-generation" digital tools à la Starfleet— organizing, connecting, and resisting the oppressive status quo.

"The future is already here. It's just not evenly distributed yet." So goes the saying attributed to author William Gibson. If that is the case, then what will it take to *redistribute the future*? The first step, I think, is to reckon with *who* and *what* currently monopolize the space to envision the future, hoard the ability to dream, and privatize the resources it takes to materialize our imagination. After reckoning comes igniting the power to imagine other ways of organizing social life and building a world in which everyone can thrive.

In cities, towns, and villages across the world, people are organizing mutual aid and community programs, even as they live-tweet protests and demonstrations against police violence, attracting more people to their cause. Close to home, minister, organizer, and scholar nyle fort established Newark Books & Breakfast, a monthly program for local youth and families. One of many contemporary riffs on the Panthers' Free Breakfast Program, which was originally geared toward schoolchildren, it invites community members from five to eighty-five to gather, share resources, and break bread together. These initiatives are working to regenerate the body politic, one neighborhood, one connection at a time.

When I attended Books & Breakfast in Newark, I read a story called *Fly, Eagle, Fly: An African Tale*, which involves a farmer saving an eagle chick from a ledge, and then raising the eagle among his chickens. "Look—it *walks* like a chicken, it *eats* like a chicken. It *thinks* like a chicken. *Of course* it's a chicken!" But then a friend of the farmer visits and sees the eagle clucking in the courtyard, limiting itself to terrestrial life when it has the capacity to soar. And so, the farmer's friend tries in vain to convince the farmer, but then eventually turns to the bird itself: "You are not a chicken, but an eagle. You belong not to the earth but to the sky. Fly, Eagle, fly!" Eventually, after much back and forth, trial and error, the eagle wings its flight, but only once it focused intently on the rising sun and let the wind carry it up and up.

Looking on the eager faces of the children sitting shoulder to shoulder, some on the floor, others wiggling two to a seat, we pondered the meaning of the parable: Who we *imagine* ourselves to be matters a great deal to who we become. And extending the metaphor: There will always be those who overlook our abilities and try to keep us in place. But, like the friend, we can lift each other up, and soar.

Imagination is the central

formative agency in human society. . . .

It's because we can imagine different futures

that we can struggle against the present state of things.

—Ngũgĩ wa Thiong'o

CHAPTER FIVE

IMAGINING THE FUTURE

———

"Robot Dogs Take Another Step Towards Deployment at the Border," announced a press release describing a partnership between U.S. Customs and Border Protection and Philadelphia-based Ghost Robotics to "breed" a 100-pound robot dog to act as a ground drone, outfitted with multiple cameras and sensors, to patrol the Mexico-U.S. border. As one news report in February 2022 put it, "The photos look like a scene out of science fiction."

Then that November, the San Francisco Board of Supervisors approved the use of killer robot dogs by the police department in what they deem emergency situations. Public outrage was swift—protesters outside city hall holding signs with messages like "Armed Robots Aren't the Answer" and fierce backlash online, including opposition by the American Civil Liberties Union, among others. A week later the board reversed its decision, withdrawing its support of robot police dogs, although the police department is still authorized to deploy unarmed robots and SFPD spokesmen say they may resubmit the proposal.

For at least a century, mechanical dogs have captured the popular imagination. One of the earliest depictions is from a September 1923 issue of *Practical Electrics*, a hobbyist magazine, whose cover shows "a man leading an 'electric dog' by a cane while a woman and boy look on." The accompanying article explains to readers how they can construct one themselves. At the 1939 World's Fair in New York, Westinghouse Electric Corporation displayed Sparko, a 65-pound aluminum-skinned dog composed of "electrical nerves and mechanical muscles." Sparko was designed to walk, bark, sit, and even wag its tail.

In the 1980s, I grew up watching *The Jetsons*, a cartoon that first aired in the '60s and followed the day-to-day exploits of George, Jane, Judy, Elroy Jetson, and their robot maid, Rosie, a nuclear family that was the space-age counterpart to the Flintstones. In one episode, the Jetsons briefly adopt 'Lectronimo, "the dog of tomorrow"—a "no-feed, no-fuss, nuclear-powered, trouble-free, electronic, apartment-approved dog." 'Lectronimo's biggest selling point? He "hates burglar masks, which causes him to ruthlessly chase a person wearing that mask." But like the *un*intelligent AI we grapple with today, from faulty facial recognition to discriminatory decision-making systems, 'Lectronimo is easy to manipulate; a savvy burglar puts his mask on George, and the mechanical pooch chases his best friend while the family's pet, Astro, catches the real thief. In the end, the family opts for Astro, and George donates 'Lectronimo to the police department.

Alas, despite exciting our imagination with technical innovations galore, those conjuring speculative tales cannot seem to envision a world without the same old social ills—theft owing to economic inequity and policing used to punish the poor. Instead, tech fixes for social problems continue to be touted and financed in fictional worlds and applied to the one we currently inhabit. Indeed, the most prominent sign at the San Francisco protests mentioned above was printed on a long neon cloth in red and black letters: "We Saw That Movie . . . No Killer Robots."

Still, tech evangelists continue to sell us automated solutions. According to the U.S. Department of Homeland Security Science and Technology's press release, robotic dogs can shield humans from multiple threats—harsh landscapes, temperature extremes, human trafficking, and drug smuggling among them. But *which humans* exactly? Certainly not economic refugees, migrants, and asylum seekers fleeing north, and residents of border communities for whom exposure to these ground drones represents yet another life-threatening hazard.

"This really felt like a slap in the face," says Vicki Gaubeca, director of the Southern Border Communities Coalition. "This certainly seems like it's something that's built for something very aggressive, like the theaters of war, rather than in a community."

But, for the CEO of Ghost Robotics, Jiren Parikh, such concerns are unwarranted: "Do we really think we're going to start weaponizing robots? It's silly to do that. I don't think that's in the DNA of America either."

But the United States is the largest military power in the *history* of the world, with a budget of $858 billion in 2023. It spends more on national defense than India, China, Russia, Saudi Arabia, the United Kingdom, South Korea, Germany, France, and Japan combined. The U.S. also has "the most advanced military technology the world has ever witnessed." So, what's that about the *DNA of America*?

Proponents of tech fixes for managing political and economic inequity and policing the response of oppressed people attempting to

navigate hostile conditions must engage in a kind of doublespeak—
hyping up the promise of technology and playing down the social
costs. They choose to ignore the fact that migrants (and anyone profiled as a migrant) are hunted down, harassed, detained, and killed
by agents of the state and vigilante groups on the border every day,
if they have not already succumbed to treacherous conditions—
drowning, dehydration, falling off tall segments of the border wall.
These, of course, are not the humans nor the conditions for which
robotic dogs were designed.

"Border communities already feel over-surveilled, over-
militarized, and yet they trot out this new technology and boast
about it at a time when families are worried about how to get food
on their tables and inflation," says Gaubeca. "And it completely dis-
regards the border communities as a community. It's like they fail to
acknowledge that we're human beings on both sides."

More accurately reflecting the threat felt by many, a 2017 episode of *Black Mirror*, titled "Metalhead," depicts wild robotic dogs
that spray shrapnel trackers, and chase and kill the only remain-
ing humans who have managed to survive in the barren landscape.
The machine is "unforgiving. It tracks, it sees, it hears. It can push
itself back to standing and adapt to specialized weapons. It recharges
using solar power." When video footage of NYPD officers walking out of an apartment building alongside robotic dogs went viral,
viewers quickly likened them to the dystopian automata in "Metalhead." While public backlash initially forced the NYPD to cancel
its contract with the company, Boston Dynamics, that built the dog,
now under the ignoble leadership of Mayor Eric Adams, the robotic
police canines are back.

But what many who viewed the episode may not have known is

that, this time, fact had inspired fiction: "Metalhead" show writers had ripped a page from Boston Dynamics' design, and footage of the company's dogs had inspired the deadly machines that appeared on-screen. *Black Mirror* creator Charlie Brooker was struck by their strange mix of vulnerability and imperviousness. "There's something very creepy watching them where they get knocked over, and they look sort of pathetic laying there, but then they slowly manage to get back up," he said.

Interestingly, too, the first draft of the episode briefly depicts a human operator in a far-off locale controlling the killer machines, but in simplifying the narrative, the writers decided not to provide any backstory. Nevertheless, we return to the humans behind the screen and the question of whose imaginations animate our physical and digital worlds.

To counter prevailing border imaginaries, architect Fernando Romero broke through the concept of the border. He designed a binational border city, incorporating detailed plans for connecting industries and communities that address shared land and energy use and transportation like express trains, buses, and bikes.

Relatedly, in his book *Borderwall as Architecture: A Manifesto for the U.S.-Mexico Boundary*, Ronald Rael has reimagined and repurposed dozens of kinds of walls, many of which begin with the simple "What if?" that is at the heart of imagining different worlds.

Rather than electrifying the border wall to kill anyone trying to cross over it, as presidential hopeful Herman Cain proposed in 2011, Rael asks, "What if some of the funds currently used to maintain the borderwall were reallocated for the construction of energy infrastructure along the border?" What if, instead of the $333.5 million used to build an eighty-seven-mile stretch of border wall between the Arizona cities of Nogales and Douglas, solar farms producing sixty megawatts of electricity could be built, powering forty thousand households in "energy-hungry cities of the Southwest?" His work is a reminder that not only should we critique the world as it is, but we should reimagine it for what it can be.

Rael also drew up plans for an Ambos Nogales Binational Library on the Mexico-U.S. border. There, people would share information and knowledge, and the border would become nothing more than a bookshelf allowing for "transnational exchanges of books, ideas, and knowledge." Sound too far-fetched?

Well, Rael's design is based on an actual structure, the Haskell Free Library and Opera House, built in 1904 on the Canada-U.S. border between Stanstead, Quebec, and Derby Line, Vermont. The front door is in the United States, while the circulation desk and all the books are in Canada. In the opera house on the second floor, the audience sits in the United States to watch a production performed in Canada. Interestingly, the first performance, on June 7, 1904, was a show by the blackface Columbian Minstrels—a reminder that (white) internationalism and creativity can comfortably coexist with antiblackness.

Moreover, the Haskell Library demonstrates how racist geopolitics—porous borders to the north and militarized borders to the south—routinely limit our social imagination. There is nothing inherently far-fetched about a binational library, except perhaps, when that inventiveness encompasses people and communities that, due to race, region, religion, and other markers of difference, have been cast outside the category of fully human.

Rael's most well-known intervention (with fellow architect Virginia San Fratello and the Colectivo Chopeke) is a teeter-totter that cuts across the Mexico-U.S. border, where the actions on one side have a direct consequence on what happens on the other side. For Rael, *Teeter-Totter Wall* "is the best way to represent the mutually dependent relationship between the United States and Mexico . . . the interdependency between two countries . . . whose economic success literally hinges upon their relationship with each other."

The teeter-totter also returns us to the importance of play—not simply as an escape from the harsh realities of the world but as a confrontation with our unavoidable interdependence. When it came to the *Teeter-Totter Wall* installation—three bright pink seesaws that Rael and San Fratello erected on an eighteen-foot-high stretch of the border in the desert between Ciudad Juárez and El Paso in 2019—it was the first time Rael implemented one of his many border designs.

Although images from the scene went viral, including drone footage of children on both sides bouncing up and down, critic Max Pearl was not so enamored, calling it "tragedy porn masquerading as protest art . . . a spectacle of sentimentality." His view is that, as a purely symbolic, feel-good exercise, *Teeter-Totter Wall* does not inspire viewers to take meaningful action to change violent and dehumanizing immigration policies. Instead, we may feel sympathy, feign outrage, "like" and share images of children playing, but then go on about our day. Or, maybe not.

Perhaps the installation invites more people to ask who and what are responsible for the violence of the border, who benefits from it, and how do we participate in naturalizing these divisions. Perhaps the violent arbitrariness of borders will spark greater outrage and lead more people to show up at rallies against Immigration and Customs Enforcement, or join racial and economic justice campaigns led

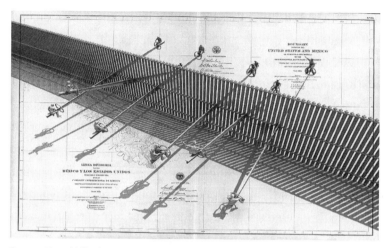

Source: Ronald Rael, *Teeter-Totter Wall*.

by organizations like Mijente, or petition their city council to designate their town a sanctuary, or call their legislators to advocate for the Dream Act. Maybe, just maybe.

I want us to consider, What are the risks of calling the teeter-totter a spectacle, or, to use another term often applied to such artistic gestures, "performative?" Could seeing the border differently denaturalize our collective commonsense and ignite more people to think, feel, and act? As a guest on the podcast *Rebel Steps*, educator Mariame Kaba noted,

> I'm actually super bored with the concept of performativity. . . . I believe in co-strugglers and I believe in coworkers and I believe in solidarity. And I believe we need more people all the time in all of our work, in all of our movements, in all of our struggles. And I think the question is, how do we get folks to struggle alongside us and with us. . . . I'm an incredibly curious person, and I feel like that's a huge help in finding yourself connected to struggles, is be

super curious, come with what you know, be willing to learn, and be willing to be transformed in the service of the work.

The point is that writing off artistic interventions as mere spectacle or performative dismisses how creative works can spark counter-imaginaries that have the potential to dream bigger and materialize into concrete changes. Angela Y. Davis addressed this issue when asked about the relationship between art and politics:

> I think that art is able to reach people in a way that didactic conversations often don't.
>
> As a graduate student, I studied extensively the philosophical relationship between aesthetics and politics. . . . And of course, art involves the imagination. And if we believe that revolutions are possible, then we have to be able to imagine different modes of being, different ways of existing in society, different social relations. In this sense art is crucial. Art is at the forefront of social change. Art often allows us to grasp what we cannot yet understand.

Perhaps, then, images of children playing across arbitrary and violent political borders is less spectacle and more an invitation to reflect deeper on humanity's interdependence.

The fact remains, Rael's visualizations stand in stark contrast to the eugenic imagination that is codified in U.S. and European immigration policies and the technical systems those nations deploy, at least when it comes to poor and nonwhite migrants. As writer Ayesha A. Siddiqi succinctly tweeted, "every border implies the violence of its maintenance."

Like Rael, San Diego–based artist and professor Ricardo Dominguez has spent the last few decades denaturalizing and disrupting borders. In 1997, he cofounded Electronic Disturbance Theater 1.0, a group that developed virtual sit-in technologies in solidarity with the Zapatista communities in Chiapas, Mexico. More recently, his team designed the Transborder Immigrant Tool (TBT), a GPS cell phone safety-net for crossing the Mexico-U.S. border. The project started with a basic question: "What ubiquitous technology would allow us to create an inexpensive tool to support the locating of water caches left in the Southern California desert by NGOs?"

They decided on inexpensive Motorola phones as the tool for disseminating this information to migrants. But in addition to using the global positioning system (GPS) to spread practical information, TBT includes a *geo-poetic-system* (also GPS) to spread love, encouragement, and welcome, as also essential for survival. Audre Lorde's insistence that "poetry is not a luxury" informs this intervention.

Between 2009 and 2010, TBT came under intense scrutiny and investigation, first by the Office of the President at Dominguez's home institution, the University of California, San Diego, then also by Congress, the FBI, and the Department of Justice. It was even profiled by conservative political commentator and media personality Glenn Beck "as a gesture that potentially 'dissolved' the U.S. border *with its poetry*" (emphasis added).

In the end, the situation became too dangerous for migrants to be caught crossing the border with GPS-enabled phones. "But," Dominguez explains, "while TBT did not achieve its imagined goal, the gesture created a series of calls and responses resonating on a global scale, which may yet bloom in the desert of the real." May a thousand realities bloom.

The power of unjust systems lies in their ability to *naturalize* social hierarchies. This happens through law, yes, as when the U.S. Naturalization Act of 1790 limited citizenship to "free white persons." But the law is never enough to uphold (or overthrow) unjust systems. Oppressive (and liberatory) social structures require individuals to internalize social categories and cultural meanings, transmitting them through our language and everyday behavior, and socializing the next generation through education *and* play.

WHEN I WAS IN the fourth grade, my family moved from a lower-middle-class Black and Latinx neighborhood in Los Angeles to a lower-middle-class, nearly all-white subdivision in Conway, South Carolina. Our new neighbors were friendly. One family included a girl, Sara, who was my age. We hit it off from day one. We bounced on the huge trampoline in their backyard. Their golden, furry dog reminded me of Lassie. Sara and I could play for what seemed like hours in her parents' car parked in the driveway, pretending to take road trips to Disneyland, Magic Mountain, or close by to Myrtle Beach.

One day, in the middle of one of our games, Sara turned to me and said, "You never see a red bird and a blue bird together in a tree. That's how you know we're not supposed to be race mixing." Her point was not that we couldn't play together. It was that the union of my parents—my dad Black and my mom of (white) Iranian descent—was not what God intended. Just look to nature, she beckoned, for proof.

As I think back, what sticks with me most about her fleeting comment, and what I think emboldened her conviction, was the *absence* of an image of cross-color avian pairing and the inability to imagine such commingling, despite the existence of my family living next door. Not scripture, not law, not fascist thought police patrolling her mind. But a *simple image* animating her imagination (and now mine) and naturalizing her erroneous belief that interracial marriages were abnormal. What's more, many millions of adults share her childhood belief—including the Louisiana justice of the peace Keith Bardwell, who refused to marry Beth Humphrey and Terence McKay.

It is not as though a cartoon about the adventures of purple chicks born of parents red and blue could magically transform this racist status quo. But relying on laws to change society, or assuming facts alone will convince people of their wrongness seems to me a foolhardy proposition. The stories we tell and the images we share—children playing across borders, blueprints for binational cities—matter.

So, one of the things we can all do starting *yesterday* is to actively work to topple the steel curtains and bulldoze the wire fences lurking in our own imaginations—confronting the treacherous "aliens" and dangerous boogeymen distorting how we see others and warping how we understand ourselves. But we cannot empty out our imaginations of damaging images or feign a "blank slate," à la the colorblind crowd, as if that were even possible. We must populate our imaginations with images and stories of our shared humanity, of our interconnectedness, of our solidarity as people—a poetics of welcome, not walls.

WHILE MANY GOVERNMENTS CONTINUE investing in harsher immigration policies and more elaborate forms of surveillance, a U.K.-based collective is cultivating an altogether different vision in the form of the Department of Dreams. A project of CIVIC SQUARE, an initiative based in Birmingham that is reimagining the public square as collectively owned infrastructure, it sits within the Neighbourhood Economics Lab, with the aim of forging "bold new regenerative futures that weave together the dreams of many." CIVIC SQUARE's Department of Dreams encompasses four elements:

- *Dreaming* is a way of processing emotions and information and making connections by creating "vivid stories and extraordinary thoughtscapes . . . making them a rich playground for our minds to test, to tackle difficult subjects, and to do 'impossible' things."
- *Imagination* entails consciously dreaming—playing with and building the intangibles before laying the foundation—"a muscle that needs to be exercised often in order to keep our minds flexible, creative, and able to see beyond what is accepted, known, 'normal' or understood."
- *Foresight* involves speculative design equipped with ancestral wisdom and indigenous knowledge and is "how we anticipate, forecast, envision and speculatively design together for the futures we want to see."
- *Identity* calls upon us to center those who have been most harmed by past and ongoing injustices, creating space "for dealing with trauma and grief . . . and engaging meaningfully with the future to be a possibility for the many not the few."

To live interdependently is, in part, to regenerate imaginaries and futures that greed and power snuffed out. It also involves questioning the version of "human nature" we have been programmed to accept as natural. For this reason, the Department of Dreams states, "in order to re-imagine our worlds we may need to re-imagine ourselves as part of them too. What might we need to leave behind in order to travel somewhere new?"

But leaving things behind, here, isn't about discarding all past traditions and knowledges. So much of mainstream futurist work is about "moving beyond" or "overcoming" the past, a narrative riddled with hostility toward those racialized as nonwhite or non-Western or "primitive." Oppressive structures historically erased many positive, rejuvenating, liberatory elements of marginalized peoples and cultures in the name of "progress."

A critical approach to imagination requires us to consider that the way forward is never guaranteed to be better than the present. At the first (online) festival hosted by the Department of Dreams, Indra Adnan of Alternative UK cautioned, "The ability to go beyond what is materially in front of you and to conjure up different scenarios . . . it can take us to a better place, one that we yearn for or long for, but it can also take us to a much more dangerous place." How many revolutions has the world witnessed where a theory of external change has not entailed a commitment to internal change?

Thus Adnan asks us to consider, "What is the human being that is constantly held at the heart of our politics?" *Homo economicus*, of course . . . self-serving, self-interested, survival of the fittest. This theory of human nature—elaborated in the field of behavioral economics, codified in law and policy, glorified in myths and media—is just that, a theory, and can ultimately be a self-fulfilling prophecy. The more people believe it, the more we will be it.

The Guild of Future Architects (GOFA), a global network of artists, scholars, designers, and doers of all kinds who are engaged in a long-term envisioning of a radically different future, offers a theory of change in which *democratizing imagination* is key: "Active imagination of the future is how humans guide the actions of the present and make our future reality. Imagination is shared through story and narrative—the way we design everything from the technology we invent to the social systems we implement, the norms in which we perform our identities, perhaps the mutations of our very DNA, and our perceptions of reality. . . . We cannot risk having a small fraction of our global community define the values and features of our future systems. The stakes are too high." Thus we must take seriously competing theories of human nature—individualistic, competitive, self-maximizing mammals *or* interdependent, cooperative, communal creatures.

Our theories are the first draft of reality. And the stories we tell (about) ourselves lay the groundwork for the kind of world we then create to sustain the people we are imagined to be.

Consider this tweet by Fernanda Meier, which was in response to President Joe Biden's 2022 announcement of the Safer America Plan, which sought to hire 100,000 more cops and invest billions of dollars in surveillance:

> No vaccines. No baby formula. No healthcare. No affordable housing. No basic income. No infrastructure. No student loan forgiveness. No tax credits. Just more cops.

It reflects a growing frustration with the same tired, punitive responses offered by the powers that be to social and economic crises. They rule at the behest of a carceral imagination that deadens all in its path. So, what's an alternative? In my last book, *Viral Justice*, I shine a light on dozens of initiatives where communities are developing alternatives for addressing harm and fostering repair, led by people who are most affected by the brutality of the current system.

Fact is, research piled high shows that investment in public services like guaranteed basic income, summer jobs programs, housing support, and healthcare access is much more effective at making communities safe because it addresses people's fundamental needs. These two options—investing in punishment versus investing in people—represent distinct policy alternatives, and also radically different imaginations. The first puts the existing death-making structure on life support, whereas the second aims to regenerate a besieged body politic. Which one will we invest in?

"WHAT IF OUR SYSTEMS were designed to reflect the complexity of interdependence, both human and non-human?" GOFA asks. "What does that mean for leadership models and political decision-making? Perhaps our understanding of 'survival of the fittest,' which fueled the Extractive Age, was immature and destructive. What actually makes our species fit for survival is cooperation and collaboration in managing resources—a path toward the *Regenerative Age* that honors our interdependence."

This idea of *regeneration* comes up again and again among groups working to imagine otherwise. Their world-building experiments stand in stark contrast to the proponents of stem cell research I encountered as a graduate student in my twenties. They were passionate about regenerating human bodies (or body *parts*) as an intervention for the sick, but for many of them, regenerating an ailing body politic seemed utterly far-fetched. But over the last two decades, I have been heartened to witness a more expansive set of social imaginaries materialize in small and large ways.

Beginning in the small UK town of Totnes, Devon, in 2006, the Transition Network was initially focused on addressing the "twin threats of climate change and peak oil" by creating paths to reduce reliance on oil in thousands of cities, towns, villages, and schools. Now transition initiatives in over fifty countries tackle numerous big challenges on the local level.

According to the Rapid Transition Alliance, an international network focused on the climate emergency, this work often entails "reclaiming the town's economy, sparking entrepreneurship, re-imagining work, re-skilling and weaving webs of connection and support that keep resources in the towns and villages where it is created. Some places may focus on the local food, others on generating renewable energy, others rethinking local transport networks."

In the UK, that looks like a transition group in Brixton raising funds to install the country's "first inner-city, community-owned power station." In Los Angeles, close to the neighborhood I grew up in, a group called Environmental Change-Makers, founded in 2005, created community gardens and a large adobe-and-cob bread and pizza oven, where they have "taught food-gardening classes, crafted solar cookers, built Little Free Libraries, and more." This group also publicizes their *failed* initiatives, like advocating with other organizations for a "GMO-free Los Angeles." Failure, after all, is an inevitable part of any transition . . . an invitation to learn, adapt, and persevere.

And while the Transition Network is a "self organising, even chaotic and certainly creative space [so] that anyone can join at any time," they also ground their work in a simple, twelve-step guide for reducing energy consumption, which can be adapted in any community. Taken together, one of the things that draws so many people to the transition movement is that they "feel like they are creating a new story for their place."

Meanwhile, the dominant story told by techno-utopianists to lull us to sleep is that the world's major crises can be solved with even *more* investment in their energy-intensive digital dreams, which usually also means *less* public participation and collective dreaming.

TAKE ONE OF MANY techno-utopian pronouncements that recently caught my attention: "As fossil fuel use continues apace and a hotter planet edges close . . . sun dimming tech heats up." For just a few billion dollars each year, special planes could be deployed to spray chemicals into the atmosphere that are designed to deflect some of the sun's warmth. The fancy term for the procedure is *stratospheric aerosol injection* (SAI), and it would have a similar effect to what happens after a volcanic eruption, with the sky darkening as a result.

This planet-cooling technology is just one of many interventions being developed by those working in the field of geoengineering. And while proponents make a convincing case that the speed at which the earth is warming requires swift and drastic interventions, the uncertainties and new dangers posed by geoengineering are many.

For instance, SAI could cause "potential shifts in rainfall patterns that could spur worsening hunger to rapid, uncontrollable temperature rise if the technology's use is suddenly stopped." Not to mention, routine deployments of sun-dimming tech could "give climate polluters an unwarranted green-light to carry on." If we are not careful, these tech fixes could prolong and exacerbate social and ecological crises. So, what to do?

Vandana Shiva, whose critique of space colonization I noted earlier in the book, is among those seeding an imagination grounded in human and ecological interdependence, and has spearheaded numerous initiatives over several decades, including seed banks to preserve the biodiversity of food crops in India and around the world. Shiva is a fierce advocate of food sovereignty and "seed freedom" and has pushed back against the death-dealing dominance of companies like Monsanto and Bayer that patent and sell seeds. She calls them "cartels" because of how these companies bypass the regulatory structures in sovereign nation-states to sell genetically engineered seeds to poor farmers, who then become permanently indebted to them. But the danger posed by these cartels goes far beyond genetically engineering their seeds, in that they are threatening the centuries-long interdependence between humans and all other living things. In Shiva's words,

> The Monsantos and Bayers of the world are *imagining an agriculture* without farmers, farming without farmers, farming with drones . . . farming with robots, farming with artificial intelligence. They're talking about digital agriculture where you don't need people. But that means no one to care for the land, because "agriculture" means care for the land.

Rather than approach farming as a custodial relationship, one characterized by regeneration, not extraction, the cartels are crafting "fictions of financial multiplication," in which ecological interdependence is written out of the story. Shiva calls out tech moguls like Bill Gates, who, she says, approach life "like a Word program and can be chopped, and cut, and pasted" rather than "an amazing complexity of self-organization . . . autopoiesis . . . writing your own

poetry, that's what life does." Again, we bear witness to two competing worldviews—life as property or life as poetry—and one of these
is directly responsible for the planetary crises we now face.

In her book *Oneness vs. the 1%: Shattering Illusions, Seeding Freedom*, Shiva not only challenges the imagined separation between
humans and nature, but presents a vision of oneness that is completely
at odds with the reigning eugenics imagination in which "connectivity" is a euphemism for predatory inclusion. Predatory inclusion is
where institutions take advantage of discriminatory pasts by providing access to excluded groups while imposing onerous terms as the
price of admission. For Shiva, oneness is not some vague platitude
or principle but a reality that can and should shape all areas of life.
It is a recognition of our interconnectedness with the earth and one
another, so that "unless we live with that consciousness . . . we are
going to destroy ourselves."

The problem we face is not the imposition of technological
solutions, and specifically artificial intelligence, onto a pure and
untouched "nature," but a narrow definition of what even counts
as technology or intelligence. The harms rain down not upon some
pristine nature but on a dynamic and diverse array of what philosopher of science Donna Haraway terms "naturecultures." An orientation that has long existed among Indigenous and Africana peoples,
an appreciation for a deeply intertwined natureculture disrupts Car-
tesian dualisms of all kinds—"mind/body, self/other, subject/object,
nature/culture, matter/spirit, [and] reason/emotion." It is a framework that not only rejects a limiting Western worldview but also
invites us to enter *a world where many worlds fit*, un mundo donde
quepan muchos mundos.

In her article "The Power of Lo-TEK: A Design Movement to Rebuild Understanding of Indigenous Philosophy and Vernacular Architecture," Julia Watson does not mince words when addressing the warped stories of western modernity: "Three hundred years ago, intellectuals of the European Enlightenment constructed a mythology of technology. Influenced by a confluence of humanism, colonialism, and racism, the mythology ignored local wisdom and indigenous innovation, deeming it primitive. . . . Today, the legacy of this mythology haunts us." Indeed. It plagues technology platforms that extract and profit from the data we produce online. It warps machine-learning programs that attempt to predict and control every aspect of our lives. This *mythology*, from the Greek "story of the people," also guides many engineering interventions for climate change.

While we like to think of human history as a story of innovation and progress, we so-called moderns are guided by a dominant mythology, or social fictions, that fail to embrace our interdependence with one another and the world around us. Indeed, "while we are drowning in an Age of Information, we are starving for wisdom."

Watson, by profiling over a hundred examples of Lo-TEK structures (*Lo* for "local" and *TEK* for "traditional ecological knowledge") across four ecosystems and numerous countries, challenges the dominant story we tell about who "we" are vis-à-vis our ancestors and in relation to "traditional" peoples—whom Watson recasts as innovators. Popular representations of Indigenous cultures, whether in Hollywood or in school textbooks, depict them as "less advanced" and "*low*-tech," if not also pejoratively as "backward" and "dying out." Yet their innovations are precisely what could slow or even reverse the social and ecological devastation wrought by advanced capitalist societies.

Lo-TEK designs are agile instead of fixed, constructed to work symbiotically and sustainably with complex ecosystems, rather than hard and homogenous like more recently conceived structures. From the *living bridges* made of trainable roots of rubber trees constructed over centuries by the Khasi tribe in Meghalaya, India, to Aboriginal *pyro technology* in Australia (and used among Indigenous communities around the world), where fire is used to improve the soil, clear debris, and protect from wildfires, to *aquatic communities* like the Ma'dan, who have developed a floating housing and island system made from a single species of reed in the southern wetlands of Iraq—these are all forms of soft and sustainable infrastructure that are animated by a radically different imagination of our relationship with nature, one characterized by "symbiosis not superiority."

This is not simply a matter of integrating two approaches, high-tech and Lo-TEK, where the former is characterized by extraction and domination and the latter by regeneration and interdependence. The former is *killing* us—from deadly wildfires to devastating floods. If humanity does not embrace and adapt ancient Lo-TEK innovations for all our pressing social and ecological crises, we are continuing to place ourselves in peril.

When it comes to climate change, in particular, we need to invest in soft systems instead of hard infrastructures, biodiversity instead of high-tech homogenous structures, symbiotic designs instead of unsustainable, extractive schemes. Our collective survival does not depend only on ancient approaches that already exist; we must also hone speculative methods, some of which grow out of the vibrant imaginaries found in Afrofuturism and Indigenous futurism—futures that are buried in the fertile soil of our past.

Talk of "tech innovation" often brings to mind images of *settling* the future—cast as white, male, cisgender, able-bodied, if not also "enhanced" and post-human. Indigenous and racialized peoples, who know all too well what it means to live in a dystopian present, get suspended in time, never imagined among those peopling the future.

Afrofuturism names a centuries-old artistic and literary tradition and an ongoing social and political praxis that upend the whitewashing of the past and future by creating stories, images, films, and communities around the simple idea that *Black people are in the future*. The most popular depiction of Afrofuturism is probably the box-office smash *Black Panther*, which hit the big screen in 2018, bringing in over $1.3 billion and becoming the ninth-highest grossing movie of *all* time. Beyond the limelight, Afrofuturism permeates not only more indie creative works but also social movements and policy initiatives that, according to artist, activist, and lawyer Rasheedah Phillips, "work to extend, preserve, expand, and protect community time and space."

Likewise, in coining the term *Indigenous futurisms*, Anishinaabe scholar Grace Dillon reflects on how "Native, First Nations, and other Indigenous authors and creators . . . speak back to the colonial tropes of science fiction" (and, I would add, science). Indigenous futurism "advocates for the sovereign. It dares to let Indigenous creators define themselves and their world not just as speaking back to colonialism, but as existing in their own right. That is not to say that the past is ignored, but rather that it is folded into the present, which is folded into the future—a philosophical wormhole that renders the very definitions of time and space *fluid in the imagination.*" A fluid, decolonial imagination is exactly what is needed in the face of fixed tropes of progress and innovation that seek to colonize our very conception of how to craft worlds in which we can all thrive.

At Concordia University in Canada, the Initiative for Indigenous Futures asks, "*What futures do we want to imagine and create* for our Aboriginal communities?" Led by Jason Edward Lewis, a professor and digital media artist of Cherokee, Hawaiian, and Samoan descent, the initiative has launched the Indigenous Digital Art Archive "to organize, care for, and make accessible the records of Indigenous digital artists." It also includes a symposium series and residency for Indigenous artists, whose participants have gone on to create performances, video games, VR works, and a sealskin space suit, among other creations.

One of the components I really love about the Initiative for Indigenous Futures is the Skins Workshop series, in which Indigenous youth develop "critical, creative and technical skills . . . [to] adapt stories from their community into experimental digital media" such as video games, machinima, and 3D printing. One of the goals of the workshop is to encourage youth "to envision themselves in the future while drawing from their heritage . . . showing them that they can be producers, not just consumers" of these technologies.

Taken together, the Initiative for Indigenous Futures creates a forum for communities to reflect on where they see themselves *intergenerationally* (not individually!) "in five, ten, even twenty generations," and develop strategies to get there. It allows them to "explore the cultural, conceptual, creative and technical dimensions of the 'future imaginary,' encouraging young Aboriginal people to be fully empowered digital Natives with the confidence to craft a future of their choosing." The Initiative for Indigenous Futures stands in stark contrast to the Googly-eyed vision of Sidewalk Labs, which we discussed in the previous chapter, especially when it comes to genuinely centering the insights of Indigenous and other oppressed communities.

A FEW MONTHS before I turned fifteen, my family packed up our three-bedroom house on Longwood Lane, in the Pinecrest subdivision on the outskirts of Conway, South Carolina, and moved to Majuro, Marshall Islands, in the South Pacific. My parents had been hired as part of a new educational initiative to revamp the primary school system in Majuro. Once we settled in, I discovered my main source of entertainment in half a dozen boxes containing my dad's old VHS tapes of every episode of *Star Trek: The Next Generation* that had ever been aired, and I was quickly hooked.

Besides *Star Trek*, I indulged in hours upon hours of reading works of fiction, like those by Octavia E. Butler, and nonfiction, like the biography of political activist Assata Shakur. The first book I dove into was given to me by a family friend as a parting gift when we left South Carolina. Elaine Brown's *A Taste of Power: A Black Woman's Story* detailed her political awakening and leadership in the Black Panther Party (BPP). Little did I know that one of the lines from the book would reverberate across my work many years later: "There was substance to the Panthers' slogan we would memorize: 'The spirit of the People is greater than the Man's technology.'" Not exactly light beach reading, but the Republic of the Marshall Islands was not your typical tourist getaway.

This was a country, after all, in which *the Man's technology* had wreaked havoc on the local population as a site of U.S. nuclear testing—sixty-seven bombs in all from 1946 to 1958. By one calculation, if the combined explosive power were split evenly over that twelve-year period, it would equal 1.6 Hiroshima-size explosions per day.

The militaristic imagination of the U.S. empire erupts from the ground and drops from the sky, taking the form of radiation fallout that is inhaled, imbibed, and absorbed by the bodies of the Marshallese: cancers, congenital disabilities that cause babies to die hours after birth, and "burns that reached to the bone." Add to that the widespread displacement locals have experienced, first for the purposes of nuclear testing and now as a function of U.S. military presence.

When I first traveled with Marshallese friends from Majuro to some of the neighboring islands, I was struck by the crude inequity: Kwajalein, a U.S. Army installation, was a manufactured suburbia, occupied almost entirely by military personnel and their families enjoying golf courses, Baskin-Robbins, and a yacht club, among other amenities. "Almost Heaven, Kwajalein," is the slogan plastered across much of the island's memorabilia. The neighboring island of Ebeye is where islanders forced off Kwajalein to make room for the army base resided in a crowded shantytown with very little vegetation, commonly known as "the slum of the Pacific."

Not only that. Ebeye residents require a special pass to travel to Kwajalein for work, and many displaced landowning Kwajalein residents barely subsist on the small checks the U.S. government dispenses as reparation. People are suffering from both the history of direct fallout of nuclear testing and the unhabitable conditions in their present lives aggravated by climate change—routine floods, droughts, overflowing sewage, scarcity of freshwater, and disease outbreaks, including occasional epidemics of dengue fever and a tuberculosis rate twenty-three times that of the United States. In this way, military technologies are reproductive technologies, as they diminish the capacity of victims to thrive, propagate, and imagine their own futures.

Witness, for example, Marshallese children burying themselves in a make-believe cemetery—a reminder of how their lives are biologically engineered, not in a lab but in contaminated environments. As Litokne Kabua, a young climate activist from Ebeye, implored, "I think that the voices of our small island communities are not listened to enough. Maybe it is because big countries or world leaders of large countries across the world think we are useless because we are very small? Maybe they think we are too small to listen to? Yet, it is us who are on the frontline of climate change."

As we reckon with the importance of imagining, dreaming, and playing throughout this book, let the image of Marshallese children playing *dead* trouble you. Let's not view it simply through the frame of tragedy and loss, or even resilience, but also as evidence of the stubborn

Source: Vlad Sokhin, *Marshall Islands Sand Cemetery*. Published with permission.

human drive to *prefigure* our future, whether that future be bleak or beautiful, through play. These children, making do with whatever material is available to them, remind us that play is not frivolous, nor always lighthearted and fun. Play can be deadly serious . . . as a reflection of the past and a projection of what might unfold.

The author in 1994, with new friends after creating a mandala-like design with shells, flowers, and leaves on the lagoon side of Majuro, Marshall Islands.

Above all, play, in whatever form it takes, is a necessity. That is why *play deprivation*, which robs so many of the time and space to exercise their imagination, whether as dreaming or theorizing, is something we must confront with the seriousness we might address other forms of theft. Filmmaker Alex Rivera put it well: "The battle over real power tomorrow begins with the struggle over who gets to dream today."

Imagination, in short, is everywhere, from sterile well-funded labs adorned with signs cautioning "Toxic," "Biohazard," and "Radioactive," to neighborhoods across the planet filled with environmental contaminants, with nary a sign to warn residents of the danger seeping from the soil, water, and air. Some people's lives are imagined worthy of protection, while others are left to play dead.

Whether we turn to children playing in the sand or tech billionaires offering us solutions while they build underground bunkers to survive the climate emergency, it matters whose imaginations get to materialize as our shared future. What will it take for kids in Majuro, and the many around the world who envision their own premature deaths, to behold futures filled with joy, justice, and well-being . . . to play *life*?

"I can't believe that!" said Alice.

"Can't you?" the Queen said in a pitying tone.

"Try again: draw a long breath, and shut your eyes."

Alice laughed. "There's no use trying," she said.

"One can't believe impossible things."

"I daresay you haven't had much practice," said the Queen. "When I was your age, I always did it for half-an-hour a day. Why, sometimes I've believed as many as six impossible things before breakfast."

—Lewis Carroll, *Through the Looking Glass: And What Alice Found There*

CHAPTER SIX

IMAGINATION INCUBATOR

———

Now is the time for us to take up the challenge presented throughout this book to stretch our radical imagination of a world in which everyone can thrive, and to engage a range of exercises and prompts for creative world-building. Some are discussion-based, project-based, or speculative, while others combine all three elements. You can use them on your own for self-reflection or in group settings like classrooms, book clubs, study groups, and organizations.

Throughout this chapter, it is worth reminding ourselves that not all futures are created equal. Instead, consider the following distinctions developed by the innovation foundation Nesta:

- *Possible futures* - Highly speculative, "might happen" scenarios that often transgress widely held beliefs or principles (like the laws of physics).
- *Plausible futures* - These scenarios "could happen" based on our present knowledge and experiences within established and emerging systems.

- *Probable futures* - These are "likely to happen" situations derived from extending our present through linear, i.e., "business as usual," trends.
- *Preferable futures* - These are highly varied predictions based on value judgments, i.e., what we "want to happen."

By being very specific about the things we can imagine in the future, we sharpen our powers of discernment about what we want and do not want, identifying what dynamics are life-sustaining versus life-draining.

When educator Michelle King visited my students and me in the Ida B. Wells Just Data Lab, she sat in front of a mushroom-filled Zoom background that looked like a page from a children's storybook. Toward the end of the call she explained that the mushrooms were an homage not to psychedelics but to the mycelium networks that she described as her nonhuman mentors:

> Mushrooms have this incredible capacity to break down anything carbon-based. And they can actually transmute poisons, so there are mushrooms that can break down oil spills, they can heal the soil. And so, that is my nonhuman mentor, because I want to learn how to be in toxic situations, but not be toxic.

For me, King's Zoom background brought to mind an essay by Rebecca Solnit about how social change mushrooms up: Like fungi that seem to spring out of nowhere after a hard rainfall, social uprisings often appear spontaneous and spectacular. But as with mushrooms that grow out of a vast structure of mycelium threading, branching, and rooting beneath the forest floor, so, too, do revolutions rely on the long-term, often invisible networks of people working under the radar.

Like mushrooms, the kind of imagination that can potentially transform toxic environments into habitable ones relies on a vast network of underground connections—with people, organizations, and histories. While the following exercises can be used to stretch and strengthen your individual imagination, I encourage you to consider them in the context of ongoing struggle and study with others.

As Robin D. G. Kelley argues, "The most powerful revolutionary dreams of a new society don't come from little think tanks of smart people or out of the atomized, individualistic world of consumer capitalism where raging against the status quo is simply the hip thing to do." Rather, "social movements are *incubators* of new knowledge," and the "most radical ideas often grow out of concrete intellectual engagement with the problems of aggrieved populations confronting systems of oppression." Forging strong connections, like our mycelium relatives, will ground and sustain our collective imaginations as they evolve and change over time.

Moreover, studying and acting together toward creating a better world does not require one hold the title of activist or scholar. Often, we can be discouraged from participating in intellectual and political communities if we do not consider ourselves credentialized enough to offer something of value. Yet as Fred Moten notes, well before those designated "activists" and "organizers" emerge, small groups of people in backyards and front porches, around kitchen tables and employee breakout rooms, have been creating the critical connections upon which all movements depend.

IMAGINATION, OR "MAKING SHIT UP"

From the pomp and pageantry of college commencements to the cer-
emonies of adorable pint-size kindergarteners, graduations are a significant rite of passage in many lives. But while they honor our effort
in one arena, school, what about all the other skills, talents, quirks,
and capacities we (can) develop over a lifetime?

Michelle King kicked off her visit to the Just Data Lab with
an introductory exercise called Making Shit Up (MSU), which gets
us thinking about our identities beyond school. While it is a great
way to start almost any group discussion where introductions are
expected, it is also a worthwhile prompt for self-reflection. Using
the image of an official-looking diploma from MSU University, ask
yourself: "Beyond academics, what am I good at?"

If you are in a group setting, you can pose the question thus:
"What unexpected title would you give yourself?" You are inviting participants to think beyond the traditional forms of expertise
and credentials common in academia (PhD in sociology, master's in
public health, bachelor's in English, etc.) and instead describe other
interests, passions, and quirks.

In the Zoom chat following King's prompt, Maya typed "fried
egg expert," Payton replied "pool expert," Daniel added "typo master," Carrington wrote "animal noise maker," Nica posted "master
re-assurer," LaJayzia continued "corny joke maker." Now your
turn . . . What does your MSU diploma say?

Rather than the staid, predictable, and often intimidating ritual of introducing ourselves in new group settings, the MSU exercise allows us to poke fun at that ritual while elevating interests

and skills that are easy to dismiss as inconsequential or irrelevant. Likewise, in social justice spaces, we can take ourselves too seriously at times—deploying insider jargon and listing our commitments in a way that gives us street cred. What if we all took it down a notch, balanced seriousness with silliness, and revealed sides of ourselves that may otherwise take years to learn about each other?

"There is a real power in naming," King explains. "In many ways, I feel like we've outgrown the names of the culture that we've inherited." Job titles, institutional pedigrees, disciplinary expertise, maybe even identities tied to our social justice concerns: climate activist, abolitionist, feminist . . . What else makes us *us*? Not to say these are all outmoded, but even liberatory labels can limit our imagination.

King is one of many educators, artists, and activists who have

Source: Michelle King, "MSU Certificate of Achievement." Published with permission.

inspired me over the years to take imagination seriously and, in so doing, to incorporate play and silliness into group dynamics. She quotes the mystic poet Jalaluddin Rumi as saying, "Sell your cleverness and buy bewilderment." Or at least, give your cleverness a rest. *Why?* It can help us see ourselves outside of expected roles and apart from formal recognitions and hierarchies, even when we are passionate about our roles or enjoy the recognition.

WELCOME TO ACORN

A similar warm-up exercise I use for my classes engaging Afrofuturism and speculative fiction—but which you can use in other contexts—is what we can call Welcome to Acorn. For this one, you can ask: If we were all stranded together on an island—or if we were the last survivors on earth—what is one thing you could offer the group to help us survive and rebuild?

In Octavia E. Butler's novel *Parable of the Sower*, the main protagonist, Lauren Olamina, sets out to found a new community called Acorn, based on a philosophy she calls Earthseed. The central tenet of Earthseed is that "the only lasting truth is Change," so that as humans outgrow this planet and "take root among the stars" we will carry the seeds on earth to grow and flourish in other environments.

Imagining yourself in the world of the novel, you can frame the question this way: If you were a new resident of Acorn, what is one skill you could contribute to our community? Responses often range from the practical, like cooking and fixing things, to "soft skills," like taking initiative and bringing out the best in others.

Like the MSU exercise, this question usually elicits an array of responses that gets us thinking beyond the dominant labels—"good" and "bad"—that we often carry around with us. In naming interests and talents that are not usually evident from a résumé or LinkedIn profile, we peek at the vast and overlapping connections that make us who we are and tie us to others. These exercises remind us that our common descriptors can be constraining and pretentious, and reimagining them can provide a freedom to think of ourselves and others in new ways.

THINGS FROM THE FUTURE

Another activity King introduced to us during her lab visit was the Thing from the Future, which she adapted for Zoom by sharing the image below. On your own or as a team, select one word from each row. For example, I chose *apocalyptic*, *lullaby*, and *grieving*. Then take a few minutes to create a "thing from the future" that draws together those three words. It can help to sketch your thing or write out a description of it.

From the prompt and my chosen words, I typed in the Zoom chat: "In an apocalyptic future there is a lullaby related to grieving, I thought of a loud-speaker system that plays throughout our neighborhood every night, like the Muslim call to prayer. Except instead of devotions, the speaker projects a mourning lullaby that gives voice to the grief that individuals or the entire community may be bottling up from a traumatic day in these difficult times. The point of this nightly release is so that people can sleep soundly and dream deeply."

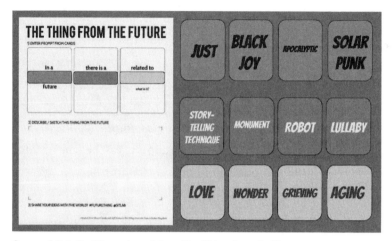

Source: Michelle King, adapted from The Thing from the Future.

In imagining this thing, I was giving voice to my desire for more ways we can metabolize our emotions and rest easy.

IN *THE IMAGINARY CRISIS*, Geoff Mulgan considers that "Good theories aren't always right: but they can be useful. Utopias tend to be wrong, but they can be useful even in their wrongness." By imagining *specific* things, theories, and practices, we can turn them over in our heads or hands, examine our ideas against those of others, and consult about the values animating our designs. Specificity, in sum, is essential for world-building.

ON THE BUS WITH BUTLER

Writer extraordinaire Octavia E. Butler observed, "Every story I create, creates me. I write to create myself." This session is mobile—inspired by Butler's own daily bus rides to and from work, from her home in Pasadena to the public library in Los Angeles: "Each bus she boards, each long walk she takes, each interaction she participates in that becomes fodder for a story cracks open into an inquiry. It slows the city down to moments and voices. Questions and answers. Theories to delve into . . . The city itself is a story, a seed . . . She's a human notebook, absorbing."

Following Butler, our aim is to think, feel, and create on the move. "Pay attention. Pay strict attention. Do not miss a thing," she implores. If you are riding solo, you can read passages to yourself from Butler's journals, essays, and fiction as you travel along a bus route in your locale, then spend time journaling. If you are with a group, you can take turns reading aloud and reflect together on how the process of movement shapes other areas of your work and life. For this activity, I recommend you bring along the book *A Handful of Earth, A Handful of Sky* by Lynell George, as it opens an intimate portal into Butler's life and mind through a close reading of her personal papers . . . a wonderful companion on your bus ride.

RADICAL IMAGINATION ZINES

If "abolition is about making things," as educator Mariame Kaba often says, then using hearts, minds, *and* hands to make things is essential. Watch this brief history of zines and adapt this tutorial offered by the UC San Diego Cross-Cultural Center to your individual or group context, by searching for "Zines and Social Justice" and "UCSD Cross-Cultural Center" on YouTube. For inspiration, you can also look at some of the zine-like playbooks created by research associates in the Ida B. Wells Just Data Lab by searching for the name of the lab and clicking the "Projects" tab.

PLANNING FOR A DISASTER WRITING EXERCISE

"What does it take to survive a crisis?" Imagining the worst that could happen so that we are better prepared to face catastrophes of all kinds is an essential part of world-building. If we do not survive, we cannot build. Kelly Hayes offers the following writing exercise for developing a personal safety plan. In her words, "Preparation and cooperation create possibilities where despair might otherwise exist." Visit her podcast, *Movement Memos*, for a longer discussion of this prompt.

1. Identify the crisis: What are the things you're afraid pose a direct threat, or a potential threat, to your immediate well-being, or to the well-being of your family?
2. Identify your immediate concerns: What are the specific things that are making you feel unsafe?
3. Map some of your responses: In the immediate aftermath of a crisis, what would you do? Who would you contact? What supplies do you need? If you don't have answers to these questions right now, take some time to think about them.

Now choose one or two secondary concerns that are bigger than your personal safety, and reflect on what you might do:

1. What resources exist so you can better educate yourself?
2. Who's already doing work around this injustice?

3. Do you have the capacity to offer concrete support and help? How can you be constructive?

4. After you have answered the previous questions for yourself, talk about these lists with friends and family.

SACRED IMAGINATION

What if . . . imagination is not only a muscle we can stretch and strengthen, or a skill we can practice and hone? What if our imagination is also a sacred space where we can connect with ourselves, our ancestors, even future generations . . . a place where poetic knowledge can emerge? Social activism typically fixates on material demands (for good reason) as a prerequisite to dismantling intersecting infrastructures of domination, and critical education usually challenges people intellectually as a prerequisite to informed action. But what about our spiritual needs?

Many of our ancestors tapped into a deep reservoir of knowledge and imagination to survive the never-ending assaults on their bodies, minds, *and* spirits. Remember that scene from *12 Years a Slave* I described earlier? It brings to mind scholar Saidiya Hartman's point that "for those bound to a hostile land by shackles, owners, and the threat of death, an imagined place might be better than no home at all, an imagined place might afford you a vision of freedom, an imagined place might provide an alternative to your defeat, an imagined place might save your life." What are the imagined places today where life is deemed sacred, despite all attempts to reduce people and the earth to "bare life"?

The Sacred Design Lab is one such initiative, addressing this

question through "soul-centered research and development." Its aim
is to translate ancient wisdom and practices and apply those insights
to society's emergent challenges. Prototyping community and spiritual infrastructure to achieve collective liberation is no small feat,
and the lab has several initiatives, including the Formation Project.
The latter provides a structure for deepening our personal connection to the sacred along three dimensions:

Inner –   tending the sacredness in ourselves
Outer –   tending the sacredness in others
Beyond – tending the sacredness of which we are a part

The aim of the project is to help us connect our inner and outer
lives, providing support and structure so that we can "gather our
people" (including at least one elder), grow our self-awareness, and
engage in spiritual formation. Among other probing questions,
it asks, "What about practices that activate my inner creativity?
What else is living in my imagination . . . if no one were around
to judge?"

Indeed, judgment—mine, yours, theirs—is one of the major
obstacles we must continuously overcome in working toward a world
that overflows with justice and joy. The first step we can all take to
unleash the potential for freedom dreams to transform this wail-
ing world into a place where all children can play is to quiet the
cynical voice in our heads that stands watch, guarding the borders
of our imagination. *Shhhh . . . Do you hear?* That is the sound of our
collective dreams digging tunnels, scaling walls, and making a way
outta no way.

BEE VISIONARIES

At the start of the Covid-19 pandemic, my family started an apiary—a bee farm. We were enamored, of course, by the crucial role
of pollinators, without which the ecosystem would be headed toward
imminent collapse. Plus, as famed poet and novelist Meridel Le Sueur
observed, "It was the bumble bee and the butterfly who survived, not
the dinosaur." But as a sociologist, I found myself fascinated as much
by bee sociality as their importance to the physical environment—an
ancient embodiment of interdependence, it seemed.

So, I began an informal study of bees, to feed my own curiosity and to share with whoever else was interested through a social
media account, @Bee.Earthseed. One of the first things I learned
about was the phenomenon of "shimmering," in which bees raise
their abdomens to form a curtain. It also raises their body temperature, warding off predatory hornets *or* roasting them alive. I learned,
too, that the hexagonal shape of honeycombs can hold more honey
than if they were shaped as triangles or squares. Most relevant to
Covid times, I learned that when researchers isolate bumblebees and
then reunite them, our apiary kin are not aggressive and introverted
as previously expected, but are friendlier and more social.

The Black studies nerd in me loved learning about Charles Henry
Turner, a Black high school science teacher in the early twentieth
century who should be considered among "the great entomologists
of the 19th and 20th centuries." Turner published groundbreaking
research on insect behavior, with over seventy papers to his credit,
and among his most important findings, Turner established that bees

and other insects were "not simply primitive automatons, as so many of his contemporaries thought." They, in fact, had the capacity "to remember, learn, and feel." As Yan Wang, a neuroscience postdoctoral fellow at Princeton University, recently observed, "The bumblebee has emerged as a really wonderful candidate for developing a lot of cutting-edge tools for studying sociality, as well as brain science."

But the aspect of bee sociality I found most striking was that due to their relatively short life spans, the little creatures I observed working during the summer months to produce enough honey to sustain the hive throughout the winter would not live long enough to enjoy their handiwork. When it comes to promoting radical interdependence, then, I think bees have much to teach us.

In his book *Honeybee Democracy*, professor of biology Thomas Seeley confirms, "Honeybees make decisions collectively—and democratically. Every year, faced with the life-or-death problem of choosing and traveling to a new home, honeybees stake everything on a process that includes collective fact-finding, vigorous debate, and consensus building." Not only do bees teach us that collaboration is how we survive, that decision-making should be collective, that we each have a part to play in creating a livable ecosystem, but also that we don't have to choose between working hard and creating beautiful, sweet things.

Bees, in short, are visionary, *literally*. When we behold the very same flower, what I see compared to what my backyard bees see is the difference between the snowy image on a vintage black-and-white TV and the mind-blowing images circulated in 2022 from NASA's James Webb Space Telescope, which can peer through "cosmic dust" to reveal the astonishing process of star birth. Bees, too, can behold ultraviolet light, and UV reflectance acts as an important visual advertisement for pollinators.

So, as Lars Chittka describes, "Bees don't just navigate efficiently over miles and learn the appearance of flowers, they can also count, recognize faces, use tools, and learn by observing each other. Bees even have emotional lives and might have a form of consciousness not very different from our own."

So, while bees are incredibly hardworking, collaborative, and democratic, I suggest that the essential ingredient to their world-building prowess is that bees see beneath the surface to the breath-taking reality of their environments. And like bees, amid planetary upheavals of all kinds, we, too, must develop the capacity to envision astonishing possibilities in our own backyards. So, let's *bee* visionary!

APPENDIX

Drawing on sociologist Erik Olin Wright's threefold assessment framework below, you can use the following questions to reflect and revise your initial responses to the discussion prompts below:

- How is our proposal (design, project, etc.) *desirable* for communities dreaming and building a truly inclusive and interdependent society?
- How is our proposal *viable* beyond "sounding good on paper," and could we theoretically sustain it and specifically iterate from it?
- How is our proposal *achievable* considering the relative power, strategies, and skills of its stakeholders?

DISCUSSION PROMPTS

You can use the following prompts for individual reflection or, even better, use them to consult with others in a group setting:

1. How do media representation and cultural appropriation shape our imaginations?

2. Think about how visual media has influenced your own imagination regarding prisons and incarceration. Brainstorm some potential practices that could bridge the disconnect between incarcerated artists and nonincarcerated audiences.

3. Consider how "diverse" representations of marginalized identities in your favorite entertainment and media can be problematic. What forms of "inclusion" do you find demeaning? What forms of inclusion do you want more of?

4. To imagine otherwise we must first "remember otherwise." How do generational histories impact our day-to-day imaginations, and how can we imagine new modes of living that incorporate the wisdom of the old and ongoing?

5. How does money/currency fit into your radical reimagining of society? How do we transition away from capital-obsessed markets to empower everyone's intrinsic value?

6. Remember, "The fundamental unit of society is not the individual, it is the relationship." Before embarking on your group's liberatory design process—in which you create a tool or intervention to foster human flourishing—establish some core community values for how you will all show up together to do this work.

7. Think about an industry or sector you want to work in or already are, then brainstorm what "emancipatory social change" would look like in that field.

8. Think deeply about your family's history and the lessons you've learned from it. Taking that ancestral wis-

dom seriously, how has it both constrained and freed your imagination?

9. What comes to mind when you think of the word *innovation*? How does it relate to your individual and your community's collective imaginations? How should we judge "innovation"—as products, services, movements, institutions, or something else entirely?

10. There's plenty of hype about artificial intelligence. What are the possibilities and dangers of these promises?

11. What does *abolition* mean to you? How might abolitionist projects help build a more equitable, interdependent society? And what are abolitionists' biggest challenges?

12. What role does your imagination play in your daily life? How does it affect how you perceive the past, present, and future? How do you hone or energize your imagination to think creatively?

13. How might play jump-start imagination and creativity for you? Where in your life is playfulness abundant, and where is it lacking? How can we foster healthy play in our communities and organizations?

PROJECT-BASED PROMPTS

The following prompts are project-based and work best when your group can meet for two or more sessions. Some of them can be used in the context of a new group that was brought together specifically for this activity, while others are more suitable for an existing group, such as a class or a community organization.

1. Develop a multidimensional playbook that includes a core vision, strategies, and tactics for a local Imagination Incubator to dream and engage in world-building together.

2. Draft an outline for an anti-racist TV show or film that includes a short pitch with a description of the main character(s), the conflict that thrusts the story forward, and any plot twists. Pitch your concept to your peers and integrate feedback.

3. Think about your hometown's infrastructure—the facilities, services, and systems that enable living conditions in a given locale. Is it artificial/man-made, rigid, decaying, or in some ways green, sustainable, and resilient? Now roleplay as your community's infrastructure-development planner. Sketch out a strategy to transition that infrastructure into a public commons that reduces climate risks while also incentivizing localized, anti-gentrifying investments.

4. Project abolition tech: First, examine one specific tool of eugenic society (e.g., police body cams or electronic ankle monitors). Then, design an abolitionist "anti-tool" that hijacks or sabotages the eugenic tool you just researched.

   ◦ Speculative add-on: Now, brainstorm how you could scale this abolitionist anti-tool across communities via networks that try to resist the carceral state. Keep in mind, scale can be about depth as much as about breadth.

5. Sketch a plan to engage your community in a process to counter a systemic inequity, and think about how to include those most affected as core participants in the consultation

and design process. Anticipate potential challenges and some tactics to overcome them for this design.

- Add-on: Corporate entities are adept at producing profitable data. How do engaged citizens measure civic, justice-oriented data? Design a metric that challenges an aspect of systemic inequity.

6. Codesign a collaborative game that gets your group engaged and primed to dream about alternative futures. The sky's the limit on design, as long as it's inclusive, adaptive, and repeatable.

7. What drives and impedes liberatory transformation? Create a visual document that forecasts different scenarios building toward a truly emancipatory future. Don't hold back—draft both your most optimistic/aspirational and pessimistic/pragmatic predictions.

SPECULATIVE PROMPTS

Mentioned earlier in the book, Kelly Hayes reminds us, "A lot of things people say 'cannot be done' have not been meaningfully attempted in our context or our lifetimes. It's easy to maintain myths of impossibility when you crush all experiments." The following activities are explicitly speculative, channeling a spirit of experimentation. For each, consider the following questions: What are the guiding principles animating your vision? Who is included and excluded? How does your vision transform old social patterns and seed new ones?

1. Draft an Abolitionist Bill of Rights to seed a life-affirming imagination.

2. Related to Lo-TEK frameworks that foreground traditional ecological knowledge: The year is 2030. Climate catastrophes have disrupted global supply chains and "high-tech" infrastructures. Strategize how your local community will transition (short- and long-term) to a climate-resilient/-adaptive infrastructure.

   ○ Hint from Julia Watson: Retrofit hard, static, and homogenous designs to leverage "soft" [i.e., regenerative] systems that draw on community knowledge as a building block.

3. Sketch an existing systemic inequity and potential abolitionist responses to it within the next twenty years. Divide your predictions into possible, plausible, probable, and preferable outcomes, then discuss with your group.

NOTES

PREFACE

ix **Acknowledgments:** My deepest thanks to Akash Kushwaha and Sarika Ram for their invaluable research assistance, Tamara Nopper for her editing expertise early on, and the entire Norton team, especially Amy Cherry and Michael Moss, for shepherding this project to completion, and my literary agent Sarah Levitt for her consummate guidance.

ix **Still,** *Merriam-Webster Dictionary***:** "Imagination," *Merriam-Webster Dictionary.*

INTRODUCTION: CUTTING SCHOOL

2 **there are three pathways:** "Gifted & Talented Students," Horry County Schools.

3 **In the 1920s:** Bruce G. Hammond, "The SAT and Systemic Racism," *Insider Higher Ed*, August 17, 2020. In 1993, the College Board admitted that "it could not reasonably claim that SAT measures academic achievement. Damage control has continued in fits and starts: recentering, the New SAT, the new New SAT, the required essay, the optional essay, the 'adversity score.' Each new iteration of the test is hustled out to fix the problems of the previous one, problems that the College Board had previously denied were problems."

3 **"and more extensive":** John Rosales and Tim Walker, "The Racist Beginnings of the Standardized Test," *NEA Today*, March 20, 2021.

4 **Without a handful:** R. L'Heureux Lewis-McCoy, *Inequality in the Promised Land: Race, Resources, and Suburban Schooling* (Stanford, CA: Stanford University Press, 2014).

4   **Indeed, the flip:** Beth A. Ferri and David J. Connor, "In the Shadow of Brown: Special Education and Overrepresentation of Students of Color," *Remedial and Special Education* 26, no. 2 (2005): 93–100.

5   **"We all have":** Ken Robinson, "Changing Education Paradigms," *RSA Animate*, October 14, 2010, 11:40.

5   **It caused a:** Rebecca McCray, "In Florida, High School Student Kiera Wilmot's Curiosity Is a Crime?!," ACLU, May 3, 2013.

5   **The charges were:** Ned Resnikoff, "Charges Dropped Against Florida Teen over Amateur Science Experiment," NBC News, May 15, 2013.

6   **As she shared:** Kiera Wilmot, "An Unexpected Reaction: Why a Science Experiment Gone Bad Doesn't Make Me a Criminal," ACLU, May 13, 2013.

6   **According to a:** Steve Benen, "Poll: One-in-Three Americans Support Social ID Cards for Muslims," MSNBC, June 14, 2016.

6   **Dismayingly, his teacher:** Manny Fernandez and Christine Hauser, "Handcuffed for Making a Clock, Ahmed Mohamed, 14, Wins Time with Obama," *New York Times*, September 16, 2015.

7   **Yet Kiera's invitation:** Jess Swanson, "Florida Teen Arrested for Science Experiment Never Offered Same Support as Ahmed Mohamed," *Miami New Times*, September 28, 2015; Jess Swanson, "White House Petition Calls for Kiera Wilmot's Invite to Astronomy Night," *Miami New Times*, October 8, 2015.

7   **Klera shared at:** William E. Gibson, "Vindicated Florida Teen Goes to the White House," *South Florida Sun Sentinel*, October 20, 2015.

7   **And she was:** Rebecca Klein, "Kiera Wilmot, Teen Arrested in Botched Science Experiment, Haunted by Felony Record," *HuffPost*, May 30, 2014.

8   **After all, "Dangerous":** Angela Y. Davis, *The Meaning of Freedom: And Other Difficult Dialogues* (San Francisco: City Lights Books, 2012).

9   **Like author Arundhati:** Arundhati Roy, *War Talk* (Cambridge, MA: South End Press, 2003).

10 **"If I didn't":** Audre Lorde, *Sister Outsider: Essays and Speeches* (Berkeley, CA: Crossing Press, 1984), 137.

CHAPTER ONE: WHOSE IMAGINATION?

12 **Sociologist Patricia Hill:** Patricia Hill Collins, *Black Feminist Thought: Knowledge, Consciousness, and the Politics of Empowerment* (New York: Routledge, 2009).

12 **I think of NFL quarterback:** Charles Robinson, "In Light of George Floyd's Death, Ex-NFL Exec Admits What We Knew All Along: Protests Ended Colin Kaepernick's Career," *Yahoo! Sports*, May 30, 2020.

12 **I think of gymnastics champion:** Brenley Goertzen, "Charlie Kirk, Piers Morgan Slam Simone Biles as a 'Selfish Sociopath' and 'Shame to the Country,' *Salon*, July 28, 2021.

13 **I think of Kylian Mbappé:** Associated Press, "France Federation Condemns Racist Abuse of Kylian Mbappe, Kingsley Coman," ESPN, December 20, 2022.

13 **I think, too, of:** Associated Press, "NFL Agrees to End Race-Based Brain Testing in $1B Settlement on Concussions," NPR, October 20, 2021.

13 **One after another:** Lorde, *Sister Outsider*, 137.

13 **I think of seventeen-year-old:** Adam Weinstein and the *MoJo* news team, "The Trayvon Martin Killing, Explained," *Mother Jones*, March 18, 2012.

14 **"Know-your-place aggression" is:** Koritha Mitchell, "Identifying White Mediocrity and Know-Your-Place Aggression: A Form of Self-Care," *African American Review* 51, no. 4 (2018): 253–62.

14 **Or, like with:** Loïc Wacquant, "Race as Civic Felony," *International Social Science Journal* 57, no. 183 (2005): 127–42.

14 **These are but:** Amira Rose David, "Black College Athletes Are Rising Up Against the Exploitative System They Labor In," *Washington Post*, August 11, 2020.

14 **Civil rights historian:** Taylor Branch, "The Shame of College Sports," *Atlantic*, October 2011.

14 **But Black athletes:** Jared Ramsey, "Supreme Court Rules Unanimously Against NCAA in Class-Action Athlete Lawsuit," *State News*, June 22, 2021.

15 **She applied for:** Mary Pilon, "The Secret History of Monopoly: The Capitalist Board Game's Leftwing Origins," *Guardian,* April 11, 2015; Tristan Donovan, "The Original Monopoly Was Deeply Anti-Landlord," *Vice*, March 23, 2017.

15 **"Aporophobia" is what:** Adela Cortina, *Aporophobia: Why We Reject the Poor Instead of Helping Them* (Princeton, NJ: Princeton University Press, 2022).

16 **Take the board game:** Simon Birch, "Co-opoly: It's Like Monopoly, but Better," *Guardian*, November 21, 2012.

16 **I like how:** Thomas Berry, *The Dream of the Earth* (San Francisco: Sierra Club Books, 1990), 123.

16 **"We are in"**: adrienne maree brown, *Emergent Strategy: Shaping Change, Changing Worlds* (Chico, CA: AK Press, 2017).

16 *The Doctrine of Discovery*: "The Doctrine of Discovery, 1493," Gilder Lehrman Institute of American History; Indigenous Values Initiative, "What Is the Doctrine of Discovery?," January 16, 2023.

16 *Manifest Destiny*: History.com editors, "Manifest Destiny," April 5, 2010.

17 *Survival of the Fittest*: Dan Falk, "The Complicated Legacy of Herb Spencer, the Man Who Coined 'Survival of the Fittest,'" *Smithsonian Magazine* (online), April 29, 2020.

17 **Strength not in:** Rina Bliss, *Rethinking Intelligence: A Radical New Understanding of Our Human Potential* (New York: Harper Wave, 2023), 26.

17 **These Old Stories:** Paul Brand and Philip Yancey, *Fearfully and Wonderfully Made: A Surgeon Looks at the Human and Spiritual Body* (Grand Rapids, MI: Zondervan Books, 1980); Paul Brand and Philip Yancey, *Pain: The Gift Nobody Wants* (New York: Harper Collins, 1993); Remy Blumenfeld, "How a 15,000-Year-Old Human Bone Could Help You Through the Coronacrisis," *Forbes*, March 21, 2020; Gideon Lasco, "Did Margaret Mead Think a Healed Femur Was the Earliest Sign of Civilization?," *Sapiens*, June 16, 2022. New stories are not only ones imagining the future but also those revising the past. Consider a story attributed to anthropologist Margaret Mead: "What would you say is the earliest sign of civilization?" Mead asked an audience. Iron tools? Clay pots? Domesticated plants? No. Instead, Mead reportedly held a human femur bone above her head and pointed out a section where the bone was thickened, noting that this is where it had been broken and healed. This thigh bone, the longest one in the leg, connecting hip to knee, "shows that someone must have cared for the injured person—hunted on his behalf, brought him food, served him at personal sacrifice." This story was first recounted in surgeon Paul Brand and Philip Yancey's book *Fearfully and Wonderfully Made*. The quotes are taken from their later work, *Pain: The Gift Nobody Wants*.

18 **Their fantastic fables:** Nick Bostrom, *Superintelligence: Paths, Dangers, Strategies* (Oxford: Oxford University Press, 2014), 102.

18 *X-risk*, **as insiders:** Émile P. Torres, "What the Sam Bankman-Fried Debacle Can Teach Us About 'Longtermism,'" *Salon*, November 20, 2022.

18 **"They don't ever want":** "Understanding TESCREAL with Timnit Gebru and Emile Torres," *Dave Troy Presents* podcast, June 14, 2023.

19 **"Saving lives in poor countries":** Torres, "What the Sam Bankman-Fried Debacle Can Teach Us About 'Longtermism.'"

19 **As philosopher and historian:** Torres, "What the Sam Bankman-Fried Debacle Can Teach Us About 'Longtermism.'"

19 **"So let's not":** Torres, "What the Sam Bankman-Fried Debacle Can Teach Us About 'Longtermism.'"

19 **In this new era:** Torres, "What the Sam Bankman-Fried Debacle Can Teach Us About 'Longtermism.'"

20 **In early January 2023:** Nick Bostrom, "Apology for an Old Email," *Nick Bostrom's Home Page*, January 9, 2023; Matthew Gault and Jordan Pearson, "Prominent AI Philosopher and 'Father' of Longtermism Sent Very Racist Email to a 90s Philosophy Listserv," *Vice*, January 12, 2023.

20 **In their new-ish:** Torres, "What the Sam Bankman-Fried Debacle Can Teach Us About 'Longtermism.'"

20 **Instead, if there's:** Torres, "What the Sam Bankman-Fried Debacle Can Teach Us About 'Longtermism.'"

21 **Torres points to a:** Mark Leon Goldberg, "How 'Longtermism' Is Shaping Foreign Policy," UN Dispatch, August 15, 2022.

22 **In *Freedom Dreams*:** Kelley, *Freedom Dreams*, 2.

22 **He explores how:** Kelley, *Freedom Dreams*, 6.

22 **Alongside a clear-headed:** Kelley, *Freedom Dreams*, 9.

22 **Radical imagination, then:** Robin D. G. Kelley, "Twenty Years of Freedom Dreams," *Boston Review*, August 1, 2022. Kelley addressed this point in a recent reflection on the twentieth anniversary of the publication of *Freedom Dreams*. He noted his purpose in writing the book was to critically engage the nostalgia involved in 1990s political organizations looking to the radical movements of the previous decades and to understand in the present moment, "What does it mean to 'win,' and why does it matter?" Moreover, he was encouraging us to imagine winning beyond the constraints of contemporary institutions and mobilizations, such as nonprofits, funders, and yes, even political organizing. While helpful, these might still seek to constrain our freedom dreams.

24 **Zach Baylin, scriptwriter:** Julie Miller, " 'King Richard': Understanding the Real Richard Williams, Father and Coach to Venus and Serena Williams," *Vanity Fair*, November 19, 2021.

24 **But Braden wasn't:** Sean Gregory, "What *King Richard*'s Story of an Uncommon Dad Means for the Rest of Us," *Time*, November 17, 2021.

24 **Undeterred, Richard crashed:** "King Richard (2021) Transcript," *Scraps from the Loft*, November 21, 2021.

24 **Finally, after dozens:** Gregory, "What *King Richard*'s Story of an Uncommon Dad Means for the Rest of Us."

24 **But Richard corrected:** Gregory, "What *King Richard*'s Story of an Uncommon Dad Means for the Rest of Us."

25 **"You gonna be":** "King Richard (2021) Transcript."

25 **Moving from the:** "King Richard (2021) Transcript."

25 **As Venus and:** Miller, " 'King Richard.'"

25 **But he was also adamant:** Gregory, "What *King Richard*'s Story of an Uncommon Dad Means for the Rest of Us."

25 **That said, for Black feminist scholar Brittney Cooper:** Evette Dionne, "Eloquent Rage: How Brittney Cooper Created a Black Feminist Manifesto," *Bitch Media*, October 25, 2018.

26 **The kind of tenacity:** Ellin Stein, "What's Fact and What's Fiction in *King Richard*," *Slate*, November 19, 2021; Alex Abad-Santos, "King Richard and reclaiming Richard Williams's Legacy," *Vox*, November 20, 2021.

27 **If, as Kelley laments:** Kelley, *Freedom Dreams*, 4.

CHAPTER TWO: IMAGINING OURSELVES

28 **"because white men":** Claudia Rankine, *Citizen: An American Lyric* (London: Penguin, 2015), 135.

29 **Nationalism produces and:** Benedict Anderson, *Imagined Communities: Reflections on the Origin and Spread of Nationalism* (Brooklyn, NY: Verso, 2016).

29 **Patriotism requires that:** Murray Bookchin, *The Modern Crisis* (Chico, CA: AK Press, 2022).

29 **What if, like:** Derek Walcott, "The Schooner *Flight*," in *The Poetry of Derek Walcott 1948—2013* (New York: Farrar, Straus and Giroux, 2017), 237.

31 **"Never mind the":** *Summer of Soul*, directed by Ahmir "Questlove" Thompson (Searchlight Pictures, 2021), 1:57:38.

31 **"The West man's":** Amiri Baraka, "Technology and Ethos," in *Amistad 2*, edited by John Williams and Charles Harris (New York: Random House, 1971), 319.

32 **When Musk's spaceflight:** Alina Utrata, "Lost in Space," *Boston Review*, July 14, 2021.

32 **As one observer:** @AnAvidTVWatcher, "With Bezos in space, there's never been a better time for Amazon workers to finally go take a bathroom break," Twitter, July 20, 2021.

32 **And in response:** "Jeff Bezos Thanks Amazon Staff and Customers After Trip to Space: 'You Guys Paid for This,'" *The National News* (YouTube), July 21, 2021.

32 **Congresswoman Alexandria Ocasio-Cortez:** Alexandria Ocasio-Cortez (@AOC), "Yes, Amazon workers did pay for this," Twitter, July 20, 2021.

32 **Scientist and activist:** Vandana Shiva, *Oneness vs. the 1%: Shattering Illusions, Seeding Freedom* (Hartford, VT: Chelsea Green Publishing, 2020), x.

33 **As Utrata reports:** Utrata, "Lost in Space."

33 **These "start-up nations":** Utrata, "Lost in Space."

33 **And yet, as:** Julia Watson, "The Power of Lo-Tek," World Around NYC, January 25, 2020, video, 13:27.

32 **Or, as one:** David Bowman (@dlbowman76), "Longtermism (as the techno-zillionaires believe in it) is predicated on a belief that an ultra-ruling class will benevolently guide humanity," Twitter, August 14, 2022.

34 **As historian Robin:** Robin D. G. Kelley, *Freedom Dreams: The Black Radical Imagination* (Boston: Beacon Press, 2002), 10.

34 **As far back:** W. E. B. DuBois, *Black Reconstruction in America* (New York: Free Press, 1998), 182.

35 **America's great talent:** Karen Russell, *Sleep Donation* (New York: Vintage Books, 2020), 116.

36 **Most importantly, *Sleep Donation*:** See also Gabriel García Márquez, *One Hundred Years of Solitude* (New York: Harper Perennial, 2006), which describes a plague of insomnia that comes to the mythical Latin American town Macondo—"a plague that makes the afflicted unable to sleep for days and causes such memory loss that objects, plants and animals need to be labeled." Quote from Michiko Kakutani, "Terminal Tossing and Turning," *New York Times*, April 2, 2014. The story resonates with one of the real-life collectives you will encounter soon, the Guild of Future Architects, whose Dream Tech collaborators ask: "Who can afford to dream? What is dream technology and how will it affect me? What would society gain if everyone started paying attention to their dreams?"

36 **"To be aware":** Indra Adnan, "Dreaming as Soft Power," 16:50.

36 **More recently:** Evan Moore, "HBCU Student in NC Argued with

Her Professor—and Got Arrested. Here's What We Know," *Charlotte Observer*, December 16, 2022.

37 **The goal was:** Charla Bear, "American Indian Boarding Schools Haunt Many," NPR, May 12, 2008.

37 **Recall education scholar:** Rudine Sims Bishop, "Mirrors, Windows, and Sliding Glass Doors," in *Collected Perspectives: Choosing and Using Books for the Classroom*, edited by Hughes Moir (Boston: Christopher-Gordon Publishers, 1990).

37 **The whiteness of:** Bishop, "Mirrors, Windows, and Sliding Glass Doors."

37 **But those who:** James Baldwin, *The Fire Next Time* (New York: Vintage International, 1993), 102.

38 **In contrast, according to:** Baldwin, *The Fire Next Time*, 101.

38 **The recent war:** Nancy Larrick, "The All-White World of Children's Books," *Saturday Review*, September 11, 1965.

38 **This is why:** Brigid Kennedy, "Texas Nonprofit Shares Bizarre Cheat Sheet Identifying CRT Buzzwords in the Classroom," *The Week*, June 30, 2021.

38 **Is it any wonder:** Benjamin Hansen and Matthew Lang, "Back to School Blues: Seasonality of Youth Suicide and the Academic Calendar," *Economics of Education Review* 30, no. 5 (2011): 850–61.

38 **More revealing still:** Benjamin Hansen, Joseph J. Sabia, and Jessamyn Schaller, *In-Person Schooling and Youth Suicide: Evidence from School Calendars and Pandemic School Closures* (Cambridge, MA: National Bureau of Economic Research, 2022).

39 **Professor of collective intelligence:** Geoff Mulgan, *The Imaginary Crisis (and How We Might Quicken Social and Public Imagination)* (University College London, Demos Helsinki, and Untitled, April 2020).

39 **As one journalist:** Terri Somers, "Stem Cell Research Focus of Meeting," *San Diego Union-Tribune*, November 8, 2009.

41 **In *The Creative*:** Agustín Fuentes, *The Creative Spark: How Imagination Made Humans Exceptional* (New York: Dutton, 2017), 8.

41 **But Fuentes also:** Fuentes, *The Creative Spark*, 285.

41 **"Teaching to the test":** Jon Henley, Philip Oltermann, Sam Jones, and Angela Giuffrida, "'Let Children Play': The Educational Message from Across Europe," *Guardian*, April 23, 2021.

42 **A professor of education:** Patrick Butler, "No Grammar Schools, Lots of Play: The Secrets of Europe's Top Education System," *Guardian*, September 20, 2016.

42 **When it comes:** Arturo Escobar, *Designs for the Pluriverse* (Durham, NC: Duke University Press, 2018), 139.

42 **Alternatively dubbed "transition":** Escobar, *Designs for the Pluriverse*, 139.

42 **Not simply about:** Escobar, *Designs for the Pluriverse*, 146.

42 **Emerging from the:** Escobar, *Designs for the Pluriverse*, 148.

42 **Rather than conceive:** Escobar, *Designs for the Pluriverse*, 148.

43 **"The historical mission":** Thomas Berry, *The Great Work: Our Way into the Future* (New York: Bell Tower, 2000), 159.

43 **Instead of *Homo economicus*:** Itamar Shatz, "Economic Man (Homo Economicus): On the False Assumption of Perfect Rationality," *Effectiviology*.

43 **"Survival of the friendliest":** Federico Demaria, François Schneider, Filka Sekulova, and Joan Martinez-Alier, "What Is Degrowth? From an Activist Slogan to a Social Movement," *Environmental Values* 22, no. 2 (April 2013): 197; Giorgos Kallis, Christian Kerschner, and Joan Martinez-Alier, "The Economics of Degrowth," *Ecological Economics* 84 (December 2012): 172–80; and Giorgos Kallis, "In Defence of Degrowth," *Ecological Economics* 70, no. 5 (March 2011): 873–80.

43 **What's more:** Ruha Benjamin, *Race After Technology: Abolitionist Tools for the New Jim Code* (Cambridge: Polity, 2020).

43 **We must rewrite:** Katherine McKittrick, *Sylvia Wynter: On Being Human as Praxis* (Durham, NC: Duke University Press, 2015), 152; Emily Anne Parker, "Sylvia Wynter and the Climate of Biocentric Man," in *Elemental Difference and the Climate of the Body* (Oxford: Oxford University Press 2021), 197–254.

44 **On July 28, 2022:** "Indigenous Protestors in Canada Demand Pope Francis Rescind 'Doctrine of Discovery,'" *Democracy NOW!*, July 29, 2022; Associated Press, "The pope's Apology to Indigenous People Doesn't Go Far Enough, Canada Says," NPR, July 28, 2022; Anna Mehler Paperny, "Protest over 15th-Century Land Grab Doctrine Interrupts Papal Mass in Canada," Reuters, July 28, 2022.

46 **"Imagination creates the situation":** James Baldwin, *Jimmy's Blues: And Other Poems* (Boston: Beacon Press, 2014), 28.

CHAPTER THREE: IMAGINING EUGENICS

47 **"Not everyone can":** Matthew Gault, "Billionaires See VR as a Way to Avoid Radical Social Change," *Wired*, February 15, 2021.

47 **"People don't generally":** Gault, "Billionaires See VR as a Way to Avoid Radical Social Change."

48 **At least 246 people died:** Patrick Svitek, "Texas Puts Final Estimate of Winter Storm Death Toll at 246," *Texas Tribune*, January 2, 2022.

48 **"We're way closer":** Gault, "Billionaires See VR as a Way to Avoid Radical Social Change." VR headsets are essentially goggles that replace the user's physical surroundings with a simulated environment, whether a movie, game, or other experience. The goal is for the experience to be so immersive that the user forgets they are wearing a headset.

49 **As André 3000 rapped:** "The Art of Storytellin, Part 4," featuring Outkast and Marsha Ambrosius, track 8 on DJ Drama, *Gangsta Grillz: The Album*, Grand Hustle Records, 2007.

50 **"The first, and perhaps most difficult, step":** Arundhati Roy, "Decolonize the Consumerist Wasteland: Reimagining a World Beyond Capitalism and Communism," CommonDreams.org, February 19, 2013.

50 **Half-cousin of:** Francis Galton, *Memories of My Life* (Miami: Hardpress Publishing, 2015).

50 **To support his:** Aubrey Clayton, "How Eugenics Shaped Statistics," *Nautilus*, October 27, 2020.

51 **He advocated:** Clayton, "How Eugenics Shaped Statistics."

51 **Turning to Karl:** Clayton, "How Eugenics Shaped Statistics."

51 **According to Pearson:** Clayton, "How Eugenics Shaped Statistics."

51 **Pearson argued that:** Clayton, "How Eugenics Shaped Statistics."

51 **As Clayton aptly:** Clayton, "How Eugenics Shaped Statistics."

53 **Today, there is:** Stephen T. Ziliak and Deirdre N. McCloskey, *The Cult of Statistical Significance: How the Standard Error Costs Us Jobs, Justice, and Lives* (Ann Arbor: University of Michigan Press, 2016), 9.

53 **As recently as:** Jason Richwine, "IQ and Immigration Policy" (Ph.D. diss., Harvard University, 2009).

53 **"The result," he explains:** Jon Wiener, "Why Did Harvard Give a PhD for a Discredited Approach to Race and IQ?," *Nation*, May 11, 2013.

54 **This is exactly:** Dylan Matthews, "Heritage Study Co-Author Opposed Letting In Immigrants with Low IQs," *Washington Post*, May 18, 2013.

54 **Even when race-ethnicity:** Danielle Keats Citron and Frank A. Pasquale, "The Scored Society: Due Process for Automated Predictions," *Washington Law Review* 89 (January 8, 2014).

54 **Sociologist Tamara K. Nopper:** Tamara K. Nopper, "Digital Character in 'The Scored Society': FICO, Social Networks, and Competing Mea-

surements of Creditworthiness," in *Captivating Technology: Race, Carceral Technoscience, and Liberatory Imagination in Everyday Life*, edited by Ruha Benjamin (Durham, NC: Duke University Press, 2019), 170. The big three credit bureaus are Experian, TransUnion, and Equifax. They produce the three-digit FICO score based on consumers' payment histories (mortgages, credit cards, car payments, student loans, etc). *Digital character* refers to "a digital profile assessed to make inferences regarding character in terms of credibility, reliability, industriousness, responsibility, morality, and relationship choices."

54 **The latter is:** Tamara K. Nopper, *Alternative Data and the Future of Credit Scoring* (San Francisco: Data for Progress, 2020).

54 **A closer examination:** Nopper, "Digital Character in 'The Scored Society,'" 170–71.

55 **Nopper invites us:** Committee on Financial Services, "Bringing Consumer Protection Back: A Semi-Annual Review of the Consumer Financial Protection Bureau §. 117–57" (2022), 97.

56 **Kimberly Jeffrey told:** Bill Chappell, "California's Prison Sterilizations Reportedly Echo Eugenics Era," NPR, July 9, 2013.

56 **This phenomenon is:** Allen M. Hornblum and Osagie K. Obasogie, "Medical Exploitation: Inmates Must Not Become Guinea Pigs Again," in *Beyond Bioethics: Toward a New Biopolitics*, edited by Osagie K. Obasogie and Marcy Darnovsky (Berkeley: University of California Press, 2018), 277.

57 **Former OB-GYN for Valley State Prison:** Mark G. Bold, "Op-Ed: It's Time for California to Compensate Its Forced-Sterilization Victims," *Los Angeles Times*, March 5, 2015.

57 **Writing about a documentary:** Cassie da Costa, "Inside America's Horrifying Modern-Day Eugenics Movement," *Daily Beast*, May 18, 2020.

57 **In the film:** Anthony Brandt and David Eagleman, *The Runaway Species: How Human Creativity Remakes the World* (New York: Catapult, 2017). The film is based on the book *The Runaway Species*.

58 **Incarcerated people, instead:** *The Creative Brain*, directed by Jennifer Beamish and Toby Trackman (Netflix, 2019), 52:00.

58 **He speculates that:** Mike Luke, "The Writers' Pen," *Tulane News*, June 25, 2018.

58 **"It just seemed":** Beamish and Trackman, The Creative Brain.

59 **The prison, after all:** Loïc Wacquant, *Punishing the Poor: The Neoliberal Government of Social Insecurity* (Durham, NC: Duke University Press, 2009), 273.

59 **Children who grow up:** Dylan Matthews, "Want to Stay out of Prison? Choose Rich Parents," *Vox*, March 14, 2018; Sentencing Project, "Research."

59 **It is not only:** Wacquant, *Punishing the Poor*, 4–5.

59 **Indeed, economists Adam Looney and Nicholas Turner:** Adam Looney and Nicholas Turner, *Work and Opportunity Before and After Incarceration* (Washington, DC: Brookings Institution, 2018).

59 **In her book:** Nicole R. Fleetwood, *Marking Time: Art in the Age of Mass Incarceration* (Cambridge, MA: Harvard University Press, 2020), 15.

59 **Fleetwood also calls:** Fleetwood, *Marking Time*, 150.

60 **While the proliferation:** Baz Dreisinger, *Incarceration Nations: A Journey to Justice in Prisons Around the World* (New York: Other Press, 2016), 138.

60 **Olatushani, who was:** Ndume Olatushani, Nicole Fleetwood, and Rachel Nelson, *Art for a New Future: National Convening 2021*, Justice Arts Coalition, 2021, video, 53:00.

61 **Like so many:** Ndume Olatushani, "Ndume Olatushani," CreativeMorningsHQ, August 14, 2014, 25:00.

61 **Starting in infancy:** Elise Belknap and Richard Hazler, "Empty Playgrounds and Anxious Children," *Journal of Creativity in Mental Health* 9, no. 2 (2014): 27–28.

62 **Paradoxically, many of:** Ariana Denise Brazier, " 'Yea. I'm in My Hood. No Strap': Black Child Play as Praxis & Community Sustenance" (Ph.D. diss., University of Pittsburgh, 2021), 31, 36.

63 **"Black children's physical":** Brazier, "'Yea. I'm in My Hood. No Strap,'" 27.

63 **By this, he means:** Loïc Wacquant, "Deadly Symbiosis: When Ghetto and Prison Meet and Mesh," chapter 7 in *Mass Imprisonment: Social Causes and Consequences*, edited by David Garland (London: Sage Publications, 2001), 82–120; Loic J. D. Wacquant, "The Rise of Advanced Marginality: Notes on Its Nature and Implications," *Acta Sociologica* 39, no. 2 (1996): 121–39.

63 **begins with:** Robin Bernstein, *Racial Innocence: Performing American Childhood and Race from Slavery to Civil Rights* (New York: New York University Press, 2012), 1.

63 **But, as Bernstein:** Bernstein, *Racial Innocence*, 1–2.

64 **Rather, given the power:** Ruth Wilson Gilmore, "Fatal Couplings of Power and Difference: Notes on Racism and Geography," *Professional Geographer* 54, no. 1 (2002): 15–24.

64 **A majority said:** Todd Spangler, "Gen Z Ranks Watching TV, Movies as Fifth Among Top 5 Entertainment Activities," *Variety*, April 18, 2021.

64 **Yet, like other:** Kishonna L. Gray and David J. Leonard, *Woke Gaming: Digital Challenges to Oppression and Social Justice* (Seattle: University of Washington Press, 2018), 4.

64 **As communications scholar:** Ergin Bulut, "White Masculinity, Creative Desires, and Production Ideology in Video Game Development," *Games and Culture* 16, no. 3 (2021): 329-341.

65 **In reality:** Bulut, "White Masculinity, Creative Desires, and Production Ideology in Video Game Development," 329, 333; see also Robert Mejia and Barbara LeSavoy, "The Sexual Politics of Video Game Graphics," *Feminism in Play* 83–101.

65 **According to Bulut:** Bulut, "White Masculinity, Creative Desires, and Production Ideology in Video Game Development," 330.

65 **Most of the:** Bulut, "White Masculinity, Creative Desires, and Production Ideology in Video Game Development," 330.

65 **A few acknowledged:** Bulut, "White Masculinity, Creative Desires, and Production Ideology in Video Game Development," 330.

65 **"It's a romanticized":** Bulut, "White Masculinity, Creative Desires, and Production Ideology in Video Game Development," 330.

66 **It gives new:** Wendy Chun and Andrew Lison, "Fun Is a Battlefield: Software Between Enjoyment and Obsession," in *Fun and Software: Exploring Pleasure, Paradox and Pain in Computing*, edited by Olga Goriunova (New York: Bloomsbury Publishing, 2014), 175.

66 **Desire and disdain:** Bulut, "White Masculinity, Creative Desires, and Production Ideology in Video Game Development," 333.

66 **He points to:** Akil Fletcher, "Black Gamer's Refuge," in *The Routledge Companion to Media Anthropology*, edited by Elisabetta Costa, Patricia G. Lange, Nell Haynes, and Jolynna Sinanan (Abingdon, UK: Routledge, 2023), 370.

67 **he also designs:** D. Fox Harrell, *Phantasmal Media: An Approach to Imagination, Computation and Expression* (Cambridge, MA: MIT Press, 2013), 192.

67 **Harrell cautions that:** D. Fox Harrell, "Designing Empowering and Critical Identities in Social Computing and Gaming," *CoDesign* 6, no. 4 (2010): 187–206, 192.

67 **"We can do better":** D. Fox Harrell, "Designing Empowering and Crit-

ical Identities in Social Computing and Gaming," *CoDesign* 6, no. 4 (2010): 187–206, 192.

68   *Archisuits* **consists of:** Grace Ebert, "Designed for Leisure, Sarah Ross' 'Archisuits' Question the Inhospitable Environments of American Cities," *Colossal*, November 2, 2022; "Archisuits," Sarah Ross.

68   **This solidaristic imagination:** Rosemarie Garland-Thomson, "Conserving Disability and Constructing a Habitable World," ABC, December 2, 2020.

68   **"I am because":** Cornelius Ewuoso and Sue Hal, "Core Aspects of Ubuntu: A Systematic Review," *South African Journal of Bioethics and Law* 12, no. 2 (2019): 93.

70   **Only $179.99:** "Bullet Blocker NIJ IIIA Sprout Backpack," Diamond Armor USA.

70   **"Ideal for elementary-aged":** "Bullet Blocker NIJ IIIA Sprout Backpack."

70   **I think about:** Yelena Dzhanova, "Companies That Make Bulletproof Backpacks for Kids Are Seeing a Spike in Sales After the Texas School Shooting That Left at Least 19 Children Dead," *Yahoo! News*, May 25, 2022.

70   **I wonder whether:** "School Shootings by Country, 2022," World Population Review.

72   **"The creative imagination":** Toni Cade Bambara, "The Writers' Forum: Toni Cade Bambara," *Contributions in Black Studies* 11 (1993): 41–43.

72   **Think of yourself:** Imamu Amiri Baraka (LeRoi Jones), *Raise, Race, Rays, Raze : Essays Since 1965* (New York: Random House, 1971).

CHAPTER FOUR: IMAGINING JUSTICE

74   **This inspired Lady Phe:** Katherine Hudak, "Arts Help's Creative Director Sutu Speaks at SXSW Panel for Breonna's Garden," *Arts Help*, March 2022.

74   **"She loved bringing":** "Breonna Taylor's Memory Is Being Preserved at SXSW in an Augmented Reality App," CBS Austin, March 16, 2022.

75   **On August 4:** Nicole Bogel-Burroughs, "Federal Officers Charge Four Officers in Breonna Taylor Raid," *New York Times*, August 4, 2022.

75   **She draws upon:** Shawn Ghassemetari, "Breonna's Garden Will Feature at the Upcoming SXSW," *HypeArt*, February 28, 2022.

76   **As Menominee educator:** Kelly Hayes (@MsKellyMHayes), "A lot of

things people say 'cannot be done' have not been meaningfully attempted in our context or our lifetimes," Twitter, April 3, 2022.

76 **In this chapter:** "Dinos Christianopoulos – Poems," *National and Kapodistrion University of Athens.* The phrase originates in a poem by Christianopoulos. Mark Savage, "Ibeyi: 'They tried to bury us, but we were seeds,'" BBC, September 28, 2017.

76 **Yet, while they:** Gray and Leonard, *Woke Gaming*, 3; Bulut, "White Masculinity, Creative Desires, and Production Ideology in Video Game Development," 337.

76 **Players can customize:** Gray and Leonard, *Woke Gaming*, 3.

77 **But there was:** Teryn Payne, "Momo Pixel 'Hair Nah' Video Game Interview," *Teen Vogue*, January 5, 2018.

77 **Remember Ariana:** Brazier, " 'Yea. I'm in My Hood. No Strap,' 54.

77 **In this make-believe:** Brazier, " 'Yea. I'm in My Hood. No Strap,' 54.

77 **Brazier noted how:** Brazier, " 'Yea. I'm in My Hood. No Strap,' 55.

77 **But, for her:** Brazier, " 'Yea. I'm in My Hood. No Strap,' 88.

78 **Brazier's research:** Brazier, " 'Yea. I'm in My Hood. No Strap,' 29.

78 **But, as in:** Ariana Brazier, "Extending Black Child Joy Through Culturally-Responsive Play," *Phipps*, October 21, 2019; " 'Play Hour' Continues Conversations of Social Justice and Play, Highlighting How Racism and Poverty Affect Black Children at Play," US Play Coalition, April 25, 2020.

79 **This "spectacular visual":** Fleetwood, *Marking Time*, xvi, 188–89.

79 **"Instead of distracting":** Fleetwood, *Marking Time*, 189.

80 **As Fleetwood explained:** Fleetwood and Benjamin, "Marking Time."

80 **In his memoir:** Solomon Northup, *Twelve Years a Slave* (Los Angeles: Graymalkin Media, 2014), 177.

80 **Russell Craig created:** Fleetwood and Benjamin, "Marking Time."

80 **Advanced as a:** "Sidewalk Toronto," Sidewalk Labs.

81 **Sidewalk Labs planned to use:** Bennat Berger, "Sidewalk Labs' Failure and the Future of Smart Cities," *Triple Pundit*, June 16, 2020.

81 **But, as Toni:** Conversation with Elizabeth Farnsworth, *PBS Newshour*, March 9, 1998.

81 **Sidewalk Labs was prepared:** Andrew Hawkins, "Alphabet's Sidewalk Labs Unveils Its High-Tech 'City-Within-a-City'; Plan for Toronto," *The Verge*, June 24, 2019.

82 **For the public:** Laura Bliss, "How Smart Should a City Be? Toronto Is Finding Out," *Bloomberg*, September 7, 2018.

82 **The presentation showed:** Bliss, "How Smart Should a City Be?"

82 **"A city is not a business":** Laura Bliss, "Meet the Jane Jacobs of the Smart Cities Age," *Bloomberg*, December 21, 2018.

82 **After two years:** Daniel L. Doctoroff, "Why We're No Longer Pursuing Quayside Project—and What's Next for Sidewalk Labs," *Medium*, May 7, 2020.

82 **They point out:** Brian J. Barth, "Death of a Smart City," *Medium*, August 12, 2020.

83 **Redbird stated, "It was just shocking":** May Warren, "Indigenous Elder Slams 'Hollow' and 'Tokenistic' Consultation by Sidewalk Labs," *Toronto Star*, October 25, 2019.

83 **The city eventually withdrew:** Abeba Birhane, "Fair Warning," *Real Life*, February 24, 2020.

83 **As Wylie cautions:** Bianca Wylie, "In Toronto, Google's Attempt to Privatize Government Fails—For Now," *Boston Review*, May 13, 2020.

83 **But despite its promise:** Kate Kaye, "This Startup Wants to Help Smart Cities. But They Don't Know Where Its Data Comes From," *Fast Company*, March 6, 2020.

84 **If it had been successful:** Nathan Ingram, "Larry Page Wants to 'Set Aside a Part of the World' for Unregulated Experimentation," *The Verge*, May 15, 2013.

84 **"If democracy worked":** Mat Honan, "Welcome to Google Island," *Wired*, May 17, 2013.

84 **"We believe we":** Honan, "Welcome to Google Island."

84 **As cognitive scientist:** Birhane, "Fair Warning."

84 **So, despite the:** Birhane, "Fair Warning."

85 **A panel titled:** Francesca Bria, "A People-Centric Smart City for Racial Justice," Panel at the Stanford Center for Comparative Studies in Race and Ethnicity.

85 **A people-centered approach:** Lucy Bernholz, Jennifer DeVere Brody, Elizabeth Adams, Renata Ávila, Laia Bonet, and Francesca Bria, "A People-Centric Smart City for Racial Justice," Stanford Center for Comparative Studies in Race & Ethnicity, May 19, 2021, panel, 1:38:54.

85 **It involves "integrating":** "A People-Centric Smart City for Racial Justice."

85 **Decidim Barcelona, which:** "A People-Centric Smart City for Racial Justice."

85 **In Barcelona, a:** "A People-Centric Smart City for Racial Justice," time stamp 21.20.

86 **"This is a":** Thomas Graham, "Barcelona Is Leading the Fightback Against Smart City Surveillance," *Wired*, May 18, 2019.

86 **Instead of "only":** "A People-Centric Smart City for Racial Justice," time stamp 26.30.

86 **As tech columnist:** John Thornhill, "Smart Cities Still Need a Human Touch," *Financial Times*, August 5, 2019.

86 **Imagining justice closer to home:** "Strong Arms of JXN Credible Messenger Initiative," People's Advocacy Institute.

86 **At the heart:** "Get Involved," Jackson People's Assembly.

87 **"Let's Dream Together":** Jackson People's Assembly.

87 **This focusing on:** Kelley, *Freedom Dreams*, xii.

88 **In *Octavia's Brood*:** adrienne maree brown and Walidah Imarisha, eds., *Octavia's Brood: Science Fiction Stories from Social Justice Movements* (Oakland, CA: AK Press, 2015), 3.

88 **So goes the:** Pagan Kennedy, "William Gibson's Future Is Now," *New York Times*, January 13, 2012.

88 **If that is the case:** Elahe Haschemi Yekani, Eveline Kilian, and Beatrice Michaelis, eds., *Queer Futures: Reconsidering Ethics, Activism, and the Political* (London: Routledge, 2017).

89 **"Look—it *walks*":** Christopher Gregorowski, *Fly, Eagle, Fly: An African Tale* (New York: Simon & Schuster, 2008), 14.

89 **the farmer's friend:** Gregorowski, *Fly, Eagle, Fly*, 15.

90 **"Imagination is the central":** Ngũgĩ wa Thiong'o, "A Globalectical Imagination," *World Literature Today* 87, no. 3 (2013): 40.

CHAPTER FIVE: IMAGINING THE FUTURE

91 **Robot dogs take:** U.S. Department of Homeland Security, "Robot Dogs Take Another Step Towards Deployment at the Border," February 1, 2022.

91 **As one news:** Catherine E. Shoichet, "Robot Dogs Could Patrol the US-Mexico Border," CNN, February 19, 2022. We are used to seeing and reading "U.S.-Mexico" border, which naturalizes the supremacy of the North over the South in this dyad. I first noticed the switch in Ricardo Dominguez's description of his work and decided to adopt the linguistic disruption to language-as-usual.

91 **Then that November:** Nicholas Reimann, "San Francisco Says Cops Can't Use Killer Robots After Public Outcry—For Now," *Forbes*, December 6, 2022.

91 **For at least:** Matt Novak, "Recapping 'The Jetsons': Episode 0–4—The Coming of Astro," *Smithsonian Magazine*, October 15, 2012.

92 **Sparko was designed:** New York Public Library, "Westinghouse - Mechanical Man and Dog (Elektro and Sparko) - Diagram of Sparko," New York Public Library Digital Collections.

92 **He "hates burglar masks":** " 'Lectronimo," *Jetsons Wiki*.

92 **In the end:** Novak, "Recapping 'The Jetsons': Episode 0–4—The Coming of Astro."

93 **Indeed, the most:** Teddy Grant, "San Francisco Cancels Plans for 'Killer Police Robots,'" ABC News, December 6, 2022.

93 **"This certainly seems:** Shoichet, "Robot Dogs Could Patrol the US-Mexico Border."

93 **"Do we really:** "Feature Article: Robot Dogs Take Another Step Towards Deployment at the Border."

93 **But the United States:** Bryant Harris, "Congress Authorizes 8% Budget Increase," *DefenseNews*, December 15, 2022.

93 **The U.S. also:** Kyle Bernal, "US Military Budget 2022: How Much Does the U.S. Spend on Defense?," *GovConWire*, June 1, 2022.

93 **Proponents of tech fixes:** Adam Isacson, "Weekly U.S.-Mexico Border Update: Migrant Death Toll, Remain in Mexico, Paroles and Caravan Arrivals, Security in Mexico," WOLA, June 24, 2022.

94 **"Border communities already feel":** Shoichet, "Robot Dogs Could Patrol the US-Mexico Border."

94 **The machine is:** Aimee Ortiz, "Terrifying Boston Dynamics Robots, 'Black Mirror,' and the End of the World," *Boston Globe*, January 5, 2018.

94 **While public backlash:** Graig Graziosi, "NYPD to Stop Using Robot Dog After Backlash Saw It Compared to Black Mirror Episode," *Independent*, April 29, 2021; Boon Ashworth, "This Week in Gear News: The NYPD Brings Robot Dogs Back," *Wired*, April 15, 2023.

95 *Black Mirror* **creator:** James Gibbard, *"Black Mirror* Creator Explains That 'Metalhead' Robot Nightmare," *Entertainment Weekly*, December 29, 2017.

95 **He designed a:** Fernando Romero, "Border City," *Archello* (2016).

95 **"What if some of the funds":** Ronald Rael, *Borderwall as Architecture* (Oakland: University of California Press, 2017), 114.

95 **of the $333.5 million:** Rael, *Borderwall as Architecture*, 114.

96 **There, people would:** Rael, *Borderwall as Architecture*, 88.

96 **Interestingly, the first:** Matthew Farfan, "History," Haskell Free Library and Opera House.

97 **For Rael, *Teeter-Totter Wall*:** Rael, *Borderwall as Architecture*, 105. See also Rael's website.

97 **Although images from:** Max Pearl, "The Terrifying Cynicism of Teeter-Totter Wall," *Art in America*, January 21, 2021.

97 **Perhaps the violent:** "Expanding Sanctuary – Mijente," Mijente.

98 **"I'm actually super bored with":** Rebel Steps, "Join the Abolitionist Movement with Mariame Kaba," *Rebel Steps*, June 23, 2020.

99 **"I think that art is able":** Angela Y. Davis, "A Question of Memory: A Conversation with Angela Y. Davis," interview with René de Guzman, Goethe Institut, April 2021.

99 **As writer Ayesha A. Siddiqi:** Ayesha A. Siddiqi (@AyeshaASiddiqi), "Every border implies the violence of its maintenance," Twitter, September 2, 2015.

100 **More recently, his:** Electronic Disturbance Theater 2.0 and b.a.n.g. lab, "Transborder Immigrant Tool."

100 **The project started:** Lawrence Bird, "Global Positioning: An Interview with Ricardo Dominguez," Furtherfield, October 15, 2011.

100 **It was even:** Drewry Sackett, "Ricardo Dominguez to Speak on Disturbance Gestures: Art Between the Lines," *The Columns*, November 21, 2016.

100 **"But," Dominguez explains:** Ricardo Dominguez, "The Transborder Immigrant Tool: A Short History," Transborder Immigrant Tool.

101 **This happens through:** "H.R. 40, Naturalization Bill, March 4, 1790," U.S. Capitol Visitor Center.

102 **A project of:** CIVIC SQUARE, "Department of Dreams," May 27, 2020.

103 **four elements:** CIVIC SQUARE, "Department of Dreams."

103 **For this reason:.** "Department of Dreams," Civic Square, May 27, 2020. CIVIC SQUARE is "a place, a movement, a community and a lab, focused on unlocking the extraordinary capability of every single one of us."

104 **Thus Adnan asks:** Adnan, "Dreaming as Soft Power."

104 **This theory of human nature:** Efe Efeoğlu and Yurdanur Çalışkan, "A Brief History of Homo Economicus from the Economics Discipline Perspective," *Adana Alparslan Türkeş Science and Technology University Journal of Social Science* 2, no. 1 (2018): 28–36.

105 **"Active imagination of the future":** Guild of Future Architects, "Gatherings," GoFApedia.

105 **Safer America Plan:** "FACT SHEET: President Biden's Safer America Plan," White House, August 1, 2022.

105 **"No vaccines":** Fernanda Meier (@lenubienne), "No vaccines. No baby formula. No healthcare. No affordable housing. No basic income. No infrastructure. No student loan forgiveness . . . Just more cops," Twitter, July 23, 2022.

106 **Fact is, research piled high:** Eric Reinhart, "Biden's Plan for More Police Won't Make America Safer," *Time*, August 24, 2022.

106 **"What if our systems":** 2020 Annual Report, Guild of Future Architects.

106 **This idea of:** Josie Warden, Rebecca Ford, and Robbie Bates, "Regenerative Futures," *RSA Journal*, May 20, 2020.

107 **Beginning in the:** "Transition Towns—the Quiet, Networked Revolution," Rapid Transition Alliance, October 9, 2019.

107 **"reclaiming the town's economy":** Rapid Transition Alliance, "Transition Towns—the Quiet, Networked Revolution."

107 **In the UK:** Rapid Transition Alliance, "Transition Towns—the Quiet, Networked Revolution."

107 **In Los Angeles:** "Environmental Change-Makers," Regeneration Nation.

107 **while the Transition Network:** Jeremy Williams, "The Transition Companion Reviewed . . . ," *Transition Culture*, November 8, 2011.

108 **Taken together, one:** "Rapid Transition Alliance, "Transition Towns—the Quiet, Networked Revolution."

108 **Not to mention:** Laurie Goering, "As 1.5C Warming Limit Nears, Interest in Sun-Dimming Tech Heats Up," *Context*, July 18, 2022.

109 **"The Monsantos and Bayers of the world":** Shiva, "We Must Fight Back Against the 1 Percent to Stop Sixth Mass Extinction."

109 **Rather than approach:** "Vandana Shiva: We Must Fight Back Against the 1 Percent to Stop Sixth Mass Extinction," *Democracy Now*, transcript, February 22, 2019.

109 **Shiva calls out:** Vandana Shiva, "Bill Gates Is Continuing the Work of Monsanto," *The Interview*, France 24, at 11:20.

110 **In her book:** Shiva, *Oneness vs. the 1%*.

110 **For Shiva, oneness is not:** Shiva, "We Must Fight Back Against the 1 Percent to Stop the Sixth Mass Extinction," at 2:00.

110 **An orientation that:** Escobar, *Designs for the Pluriverse*, 3; see also Donna

Jeanne Haraway, *The Companion Species Manifesto: Dogs, People, and Significant Otherness* (Chicago: Prickly Paradigm Press, 2020).

110 **It is a framework:** "Zapatismo," Global Social Theory; this is a Zapatismo invitation, *Un Mundo Donde Quepan Muchos Mundos*, which emphasizes "the dignity of 'others,' belonging, and common struggle, as well as the importance of laughter, dancing, and nourishing children." See also Marisol de la Cadena and Mario Blaser, *A World of Many Worlds* (Durham, NC: Duke University Press, 2018).

111 **In her article "The Power of Lo-TEK":** Julia Watson, "The Power of Lo-TEK: A Design Movement to Rebuild Understanding of Indigenous Philosophy and Vernacular Architecture," *Common Edge*, June 21, 2019. "Lo-TEK, derived from Traditional Ecological Knowledge, is a cumulative body of multigenerational knowledge, practices, and beliefs, countering the idea that indigenous innovation is primitive and exists isolated from technology. It is sophisticated and designed to sustainably work with complex ecosystems."

111 **Indeed, "while we":** Watson, "The Power of Lo-TEK."

111 **When it comes to climate change:** Watson, "The Power of Lo-TEK."

112 **Afrofuturism names a:** Alondra Nelson, "Introduction: Future Texts," *Social Text* 20, no. 2 (2002): 1–15.

112 **The most popular:** Pragya Chowdhury, "Marvel's 2018 'Black Panther' Becomes No 1 Movie on Disney+ Thanks to Sequel 'Black Panther: Wakanda Forever'," Meaww.com, November 21, 2022.

112 **Beyond the limelight:** Rasheedah Phillips, "Race Against Time: Afrofuturism and Our Liberated Housing Futures," *Afrofuturism and the Law* 9, no. 1 (March 26, 2022): 16–34.

113 **"Native, First Nations, and other":** Rebecca Roanhorse, "Postcards from the Apocalypse," *Uncanny Magazine,* no. 20, 2015.

114 **At Concordia University:** Initiative for Indigenous Futures, "About."

114 **Led by Jason Edward Lewis:** Initiative for Indigenous Futures, "Indigenous Digital Art Archive."

114 **One of the components:** "Skins Workshops," Initiative for Indigenous Futures.

114 **It allows them to:** "About," Initiative for Indigenous Futures.

115 **Little did I:** Elaine Brown, *A Taste of Power: A Black Woman's Story* (New York: Anchor Books, 1994), 137.

115 **This was a country:** Alexander Reed Kelly, "Scientists Warn Giant

Nuclear Sarcophagus in Marshall Islands Is Leaking," *Truthdig*, July 3, 2015.

115 **By one calculation:** Calin Georgescu, *Report of the Special Rapporteur on the Implications for Human Rights of the Environmentally Sound Management* (United Nations Digital Library, 2012), 14. One report sums it up: "The Marshallese are convinced that there is sufficient evidence . . . of intergenerational harm caused by radiation fallout."

116 **The militaristic imagination:** Dan Zak, "A Ground Zero Forgotten," *Washington Post*, November 27, 2015.

116 **"Almost Heaven, Kwajalein":** Shannon Marcoux, "Trust Issues: Militarization, Destruction, and the Search for a Remedy in the Marshall Islands," *Columbia Human Rights Law Review*, January 9, 2021.

116 **The neighboring island of Ebeye:** Zak, "A Ground Zero Forgotten."

116 **Ebeye residents require:** Marcoux, "Trust Issues: Militarization, Destruction, and the Search for a Remedy in the Marshall Islands."

116 **People are suffering:** Grace Ganz, "Tuberculosis in the Marshall Islands: A Public Health Emergency," *Borgen Project*; Greg Dvorak, "Detouring Kwajalein: At Home Between Coral and Concrete in the Marshall Islands," chapter 9 in *Touring Pacific Cultures*, edited by Kalissa Alexeyeff and John Taylor (Canberra: Australian National University Press, 2016), 97–140.

117 **As Litokne Kabua:** Hilna Jilani, "On the Frontline of the Climate Crisis in Marshall Islands," *The Elders*, June 11, 2020.

119 **Filmmaker Alex Rivera:** Alex Rivera, "Alex Rivera Speaking at Platform Summit 2014," Platform, November 19, 2014, time stamp 18:00 min.

120 **"I can't believe that":** Lewis Carroll and John Tenniel, *Through the Looking-Glass: And What Alice Found There* (Mineola, NY: Dover Publications, 1999), 92.

CHAPTER SIX: IMAGINATION INCUBATOR

121 **Throughout this chapter:** Mulgan, *The Imaginary Crisis*, 24.

122 **"Mushrooms have this incredible":** Michelle King, "Tech Freedom School," Guest Lecture (Ida B. Wells Just Data Lab, July 12, 2022, virtual).

122 **But as with mushrooms:** Rebecca Solnit, "'Hope Is an Embrace of the Unknown': Rebecca Solnit on Living in Dark Times," *Guardian*, July 15, 2016; see also Rebecca Solnit, *Hope in the Dark: Untold Histories, Wild Possibilities* (Chicago: Haymarket Books, 2016), xv.

123 **Rather, "social movements":** Kelley, *Freedom Dreams*, 9.

123 **Yet as Fred Moten:** Roberto Sirvent, "BAR Book Forum: Fred Moten's 'Consent Not to Be a Single Being,'" *Black Agenda Report*, July 25, 2018.

125 **"There is a real power":** Michelle King, "Tech Freedom School," Guest Lecture.

126 **She quotes the mystic poet:** "Sell Your Cleverness and Buy Bewilderment," *Technology of the Heart*, May 11, 2008.

126 **The central tenet:** Octavia E. Butler, *Parable of the Sower* (New York: Grand Central Publishing, 2020), 3, 77.

127 **these exercises:** Isa Kolehmainen, "Speculative Design: A Design Niche or a New Tool for Government Innovation?," *Nesta*, April 5, 2016.

127 **Another activity King:** Michelle King, "Things from the Future," July 12, 2022; "The Thing from the Future," *Situation Lab*. King adapted the exercise from Stuart Candy and Jeff Watson's "The Thing from the Future Redux Playsheet."

128 **Writer extraordinaire:** Taylor Jasmine, "Quotes by Octavia E. Butler on Writing and Human Nature," *Literary Ladies Guide*, August 8, 2017.

129 **"Each bus she boards":** Lynell George, *A Handful of Earth, a Handful of Sky: The World of Octavia E. Butler* (Santa Monica, CA: Angel City Press, 2020), 94.

129 **Following Butler, our aim:** George, *A Handful of Earth, a Handful of Sky*, 95.

129 **If "abolition is":** Mariame Kaba, "'Abolition Is About Making Things': Creativity in Organizing," Cooper Union, December 8, 2020.

129 **Watch this brief:** Camila Knigge Unibe, "Zines and Social Justice," University of California San Diego Cross-Cultural Center.

129 **For inspiration, you:** "Projects," Ida B. Wells Just Data Lab.

130 **In her words:** Kelly Hayes, "Planning for Disaster: A Writing Exercise," *Movement Memos*, October 21, 2020.

131 **It brings to mind:** Saidiya V. Hartman, *Lose Your Mother: A Journey Along the Atlantic Slave Route* (New York: Farrar, Straus and Giroux, 2008), 97.

131 **What are the imagined places:** Giorgio Agamben, *Homo Sacer: Sovereign Power and Bare Life* (Stanford, CA: Stanford University Press, 1998), 6.

132 **Prototyping community and spiritual infrastructure:** "How We Work," Sacred Design Lab.

132 **Among other probing questions:** *The Formation Manual: A Guide to Spiritual Becoming* (Cambridge, MA: Sacred Design Lab, 2018), 96.

133 **Plus, as famed poet and novelist:** Meridel Le Sueur and Elaine Hedges, *Ripening: Selected Work* (New York: Feminist Press, 1990), 266.

133 **It also raises:** Joshua Howgego, "Honeybees Gang Up to Roast Invading Hornets Alive—at a Terrible Cost," *New Scientist*, July 16, 2018; Spooky, "Giant Honeybees Use Shimmering 'Mexican Waves' to Repel Invaders," *Oddity Central*, May 8, 2019.

133 **I learned, too:** Robert Krulwich, "What Is It About Bees and Hexagons?," NPR, May 14, 2013.

133 **Most relevant to Covid times:** Alaina O'Regan, "Bumblebees Kept in Isolation Make Up for It by Being More Social Later," Princeton University, July 12, 2022.

133 **The Black studies nerd:** Edward D. Melillo, "Charles Henry Turner: The Little-Known Black High School Science Teacher Who Revolutionized the Study of Insect Behavior in the Early 20th Century," *The Conversation*, July 29, 2022. Turner "shed light on the secret lives of bees, the winged pollinators that ensure the welfare of human food systems and the survival of Earth's biosphere."

133 **Turner published groundbreaking:** Melillo, "Charles Henry Turner."

134 **They, in fact:** Melillo, "Charles Henry Turner."

134 **As Yan Wang:** O'Regan, "Bumblebees Kept in Isolation Make Up for It by Being More Social Later"; see also Lars Chittka, *The Mind of a Bee* (Princeton, NJ: Princeton University Press, 2022).

134 **But the aspect of bee sociality:** Silvia C. Remolina and Kimberly A. Hughes, "Evolution and Mechanisms of Long Life and High Fertility in Queen Honey Bees," *AGE* 30, no. 2–3 (2008): 177–85.

134 **In his book *Honeybee Democracy*:** Thomas D. Seeley, *Honeybee Democracy* (Princeton, NJ: Princeton University Press, 2010).

135 **So, as Lars Chittka describes:** Chittka, *The Mind of a Bee.*

APPENDIX

137 **Drawing on sociologist:** Erik Olin Wright, *Envisioning Real Utopias* (London: Verso, 2010), 21–25.

137 **You can use the following:** The following discussion prompts were developed by my amazing research assistant, Akash Kushwaha, Princeton class of 2022.

138 **To imagine otherwise:** "Art for a New Future: Spotlight on Free Lands Free People," Justice Arts Coalition, June 22, 2021.

138 **Remember, "the fundamental":** Micah Bazant, Forward Together, and Culture Strike, "How to Reimagine the World," Forward Together.

139 **Some of them can be used:** The following project prompts were also developed by Akash Kushwaha.

141 **Mentioned earlier in the book:** Hayes, "A lot of things people say 'cannot be done' have not been meaningfully attempted in our context or our lifetimes."

141 **How does your vision transform:** The following speculative prompts were also developed by Akash Kushwaha.

INDEX

Norton Shorts

BRILLIANCE WITH BREVITY

W. W. Norton & Company has been independent since 1923, when William Warder Norton and Mary (Polly) D. Herter Norton first published lectures delivered at the People's Institute, the adult education division of New York City's Cooper Union. In the 1950s, Polly Norton transferred control of the company to its employees.

One hundred years after its founding, W. W. Norton & Company inaugurates a new century of visionary independent publishing with Norton Shorts. Written by leading-edge scholars, these eye-opening books deliver bold thinking and fresh perspectives in under two hundred pages.

Available Winter 2024

Imagination: A Manifesto by Ruha Benjamin

Wild Girls: How the Outdoors Shaped the Women who Challenged a Nation by Tiya Miles

Against Technoableism: Rethinking Who Needs Improvement by Ashley Shew

Literary Theory for Robots: How Computers Learned to Write by Dennis Yi Tenen

Forthcoming

Mehrsa Baradaran on the racial wealth gap

Rina Bliss on the "reality" of race

Merlin Chowkwanyum on the social determinants of health

Daniel Aldana Cohen on eco-apartheid

Jim Downs on cultural healing

Reginald K. Ellis on Black education versus Black freedom

Brooke Harrington on offshore finance

Justene Hill Edwards on the history of inequality in America

Destin Jenkins on a short history of debt

Quill Kukla on a new vision of consent

Barry Lam on discretion

Matthew Lockwood on a new history of exploration

Natalia Molina on the myth of assimilation

Rhacel Salazar Parreñas on human trafficking

Tony Perry on water in African American culture and history

Beth Piatote on living with history

Ashanté Reese on the transformative possibilities of food

Jeff Sebo on the moral circle

Tracy K. Smith on poetry in an age of technology

Onaje X. O. Woodbine on transcendence in sports